# Understanding depression

Why adults experience depression and what can help

## EDITORS

**DR GILLIAN BOWDEN MBE, AFBPsS**
Consultant Clinical Psychologist. Lecturer at the
University of East Anglia.

**DR SUE HOLTTUM, CPSYCHOL, AFBPsS**
BAAT Research Officer and Senior Lecturer in Applied
Psychology at the Salomons Institute for Applied
Psychology, Canterbury Christ Church University.

**DR RASHMI SHANKAR, CPSYCHOL**
Consultant Clinical Psychologist at Berkshire Healthcare
NHS Foundation Trust and Visiting Tutor at the Oxford
Institute of Clinical Psychology Training.

**ANNE COOKE**
Principal Lecturer and Clinical Director of the Doctoral
Programme in Clinical Psychology, Salomons Institute for
Applied Psychology, Canterbury Christ Church University.

**PROFESSOR PETER KINDERMAN**
Professor of Clinical Psychology at the University of
Liverpool.

© The British Psychological Society 2020
ISBN: 978-1-85433-781-8

# Contents

Understanding depression

CONTENTS

# About the Editors

## GILLIAN BOWDEN

Gillian worked in the NHS for more than 30 years. She trained as a clinical psychologist with South East Thames Regional Health Authority (now the Salomons course at CCCU) and worked in adult mental health and primary care NHS settings in South East London before moving to Norfolk in 1998 where she became a Consultant Clinical Psychologist with Norfolk and Suffolk NHS Trust. She became an honorary senior lecturer with the University of East Anglia and now works part time on the doctoral training course in clinical psychology.

Gillian is a council member for the East of England Clinical Senate.

Gillian is interested in coproduced approaches to service delivery that engage with people in the context of their communities. She is also interested in wellbeing at work and how people manage demanding aspects of work and which factors they find rewarding or protective against stress. Gillian was awarded an MBE for services to mental health in Norfolk in 2009.

At the time of publication, Gillian hopes to have begun training to be a yoga teacher.

## SUE HOLTTUM

Sue works four days per week at the Salomons Institute for Applied Psychology, Canterbury Christ Church University, and one day per week at the British Association of Art Therapists (BAAT). During her PhD studies (on the psychology of depression), Sue drew on her own earlier experience of severe depression and receiving treatment in the mental health system, as well as beginning to get acquainted with a broad and ever-increasing research literature.

Sue supervises doctoral research projects on a range of topics from art therapy to staff wellbeing and mental health treatment and recovery. Sue works with the Salomons Group of Experts by Experience (SAGE), especially in relation to research consultation. Sue's work with art therapists has most recently involved leading on the research underpinning of new BAAT guidelines on art therapy for people with a psychosis-related diagnosis. Sue writes a regular *Research Watch* feature for the journal *Mental Health and Social Inclusion*.

## RASHMI SHANKAR

Rashmi Shankar is a Consultant Clinical Psychologist and a Chartered Psychologist. She is a Visiting Tutor at the Oxford Institute of Clinical Psychology Training.

After her academic training in India, she qualified as a clinical psychologist on the NHS Trent Regional Health Authority/University of Leicester Course and went on to complete her doctoral research on the psychosis spectrum at the University of Oxford (Department of Experimental Psychology). She has worked as a clinical psychologist within the NHS secondary care adult mental health sector for 30 years.

For more than a decade, she has been the Professional Lead for psychological therapies services within the Newbury locality CMHT (Berkshire Healthcare NHS Foundation Trust), where she offers psychological assessment and therapy and supervises applied psychology and medical trainees.

As part of her professional role in adult clinical psychology, Rashmi has pursued innovations in practice to deliver clinical psychology assessments and Culturally Adapted Cognitive Behaviour Therapy interventions in a multi-lingual context (English, Hindi and Urdu). Maintaining a focus on equitable access to clinical psychology services, Rashmi has developed working partnerships with local Black Asian and Minority Ethnic (BAME) Community organisations to offer bilingual outreach information sessions on stress, anxiety and depression. Based on her clinical experience, Rashmi has contributed to the discussions on diversity issues on BPS committees.

Throughout her NHS career, Rashmi has remained committed to supporting professional training and supervision. She has worked closely with her colleagues on the Oxford Doctoral Course in Clinical Psychology to develop and teach a module on 'Cultural Competence/Culturally Adapted CBT' and she has been an invited lecturer on clinical psychology training programmes in Southampton, Bath and Cardiff. For many years, Rashmi has taught CBT courses as part of the medical education in her employing Trust where she is the CBT Course Tutor for the Junior Doctors.

## ANNE COOKE

Anne is Principal Lecturer and Clinical Director of the Doctoral Programme in Clinical Psychology at the Salomons Institute for Applied Psychology, Canterbury Christ Church University, which trains clinical psychologists for the National Health Service. For many years she worked as a consultant clinical psychologist in the NHS, leading psychology services in community and hospital mental health teams.

Anne was the co-ordinating editor of the British Psychological Society's previous public information report Understanding Psychosis and Schizophrenia. Anne is also active in the media and on social media. She is engaged with colleagues in the Discursive of Tunbridge Wells project, which aims to open up debates about key issues in mental health and clinical psychology via a blog and a series of podcasts.

In 2017 she was named the Society's Practitioner of the Year in recognition of her public-facing work to make available good quality information about mental health. You can follow her on Twitter as @annecooke14.

## PETER KINDERMAN

Peter is Professor of Clinical Psychology at the University of Liverpool and a former President of the British Psychological Society. His research interests are in psychological processes underpinning wellbeing and mental health. He has published widely on the role of psychological factors as mediators between biological, social and circumstantial factors in mental health and wellbeing, and has received significant research grant funding. The most recent was from the Economic and Social Research Council (ESRC), to lead a three-year evidence synthesis programme for the 'What Works Centre for Wellbeing', exploring the effectiveness of policies aimed at improving community wellbeing and from the National Institute for Health Research to investigate the effectiveness of human rights training in dementia care. His most recent book, *A Manifesto for Mental Health*, presents his vision for the future of mental health services. You can follow him on Twitter as @peterkinderman.

## ARTWORK

Many thanks to Anita Klein and Sue Holttum for kindly giving permission to illustrate this document with their art.

Front cover image: detail of Reading in Autumn by Anita Klein (www.anitaklein.com).

All other images by Sue Holttum.

## CONTRIBUTORS

**FRANCES BATY**

**JERRY BURGESS**

**DINA BEDAIR**

**DIANA BYRNE**

**ISABEL CLARK**

**JUDE CLARKE**

**STEPH DE LA HAYE**

**ROXANE GERVAIS**

**ELEANOR GRANT**

**PAUL GILBERT**

**JO HEMMINGFIELD**

**LUCY JOHNSTONE**

**LAURA LEA**

**JOHN MCGOWAN**

**SUE MCPHERSON**

**DI MORRIS**

**LINDA RILEY**

**GLENN ROBERTS**

**GERALDINE SCOTT-HEYES**

**STE WEATHERHEAD**

**CHRIS WILLIAMS**

**Contributing Groups – Survivors of Depression in Transition (SODIT) and Salomons Advisory Group of Experts by Experience (SAGE)**

Note – We are grateful to all those who have either directly contributed or offered suggestions as this document developed. The views expressed are those of the editors and not necessarily those of the people listed above.

We gratefully acknowledge the help and administrative support of Sally Anderson, Caitlin Core, Claire Fullalove, Aaron Burgess, Thomas Mundy, Hannah Farndon and Amy Cooke.

Dedicated to Jude Clarke.

# Using this document

This document is for everyone who has an interest in depression – those of us who experience it, our friends and family, and those of us who provide services to help. It is an up-to-date summary of what the research says, written in everyday language.

Given that depression is a vast subject, this report covers a wide range of topics. The sections are clearly signposted and self-contained, so that you can focus on the information that interests you.

**Part 1** describes some experiences of depression. We hear how individual experiences are very different and how depression is a common and serious problem.

In **Part 2**, we identify some of the many complex, multi-layered and wide-ranging reasons that people become depressed.

In **Part 3**, we look at our mental health services, and what people who experience depression can expect when using these services, and in **Part 4,** we take a broader look at what can help us, and the people close to us, when we are depressed.

Addressing the issues raised in the document is a global challenge.[1] Nevertheless, we, as individuals and in groups can take action to make a difference. We argue in this report that important aspects of society have become 'depressogenic', in other words, they can lead to depression. In **Part 5** we consider how communities and societies can become 'antidepressant' (less likely to make us depressed and more helpful when we are depressed). How can we prevent depression rather than offering help only once people are depressed?

The final resources section gives details of some useful publications, websites, organisations and other resources. This section requires addition and development and we hope it will be updated regularly.

# Note on the language used in this report

There is considerable debate as to how best to describe human distress, including the experiences we call depression. Some people see these experiences as an illness with a largely physical cause; others see them as more often related to the events and circumstances of our lives and may even dislike the term 'depression' because they feel that it implies illness. However, this is not necessarily the case: the word has been around for a long time and is part of our everyday language. In this report, we use the word in its everyday sense to mean an experience of persistent low mood. In this sense, we experience depression, just as we experience anxiety, anger, or even love and joy. Throughout this document, we highlight debates about whether and when it might be useful to think of depression as an illness. In recognition of these debates, we use quotation marks around psychiatric terminology such as 'clinical depression' or 'major depressive disorder'.

# Intention of this report

Four of the editors and many contributors to this report are clinical psychologists drawn from the NHS and universities and brought together by their professional body, The British Psychological Society, Division of Clinical Psychology. Some of the editors and many contributors have drawn on lived experiences of depression and of using mental health services.

Depression is a vast topic. Our aim is to communicate some key messages relevant to depression in adults, based on published research, and to stimulate debate. We expect and hope that this publication will be developed and refined over time, with the benefit of comments and further contributions and links to new and updated resources.

This report was written before the Covid-19 pandemic that has altered our world and led to much suffering. Many of the key messages of this report seem even more urgent and the need to address social and income inequalities has been highlighted sharply by the more severe impact of this pandemic on certain sections of society (e.g. those who face economic challenges, and those belonging to Black and minoritised ethnic groups). Difficult and overdue conversations are now taking place that may help us to make different choices. Much needed change feels possible. We hope that the information in this report can add to these conversations.

# Foreword by
# Professor Paul Gilbert OBE FBPsS

'Depression' is not a word that describes just one state of mind, but refers to a whole array of different feelings and thoughts that people experience in different ways in different situations. There are, of course, some common themes to experiences of depression around the world: loss of feelings of pleasure; having a pessimistic view of the future, feeling as if life is too harsh and difficult, often with sleep difficulties, feelings of tiredness, fatigue and/or in some way feeling 'ill'. Many of the people I have worked with also use the term dread – waking up in the morning with a sense of dread of having to get through another day. Dread is not a word that crops up medically but it's a useful description for how a depressed person feels in struggling to cope with the challenges and tasks of living. Some people also have feelings of anxiety or withdrawal but others can express irritability, anger and aggression. Some people cope with their depression by drinking to numb pain others seek out supplements and alternative medicines to directly change their 'body states.'

Depression is not just 'in our heads', as beliefs and imaginations. Indeed we now know that depression can be associated with a whole range of changes in our bodies. Recent research has shown changes in parts of our brain, in our immune, cardiovascular and digestive systems. There is evidence that our diets may contribute to depression. Increasing evidence is showing that the bacteria that live in our gut can have a major impact on our mood. So depression is not just a psychological state. We are increasingly understanding that depression emerges from complex biopsychosocial interactions and that we must not ignore the body or social and economic contexts. Hence, depressed people would be well advised to be checked out physically in case of undetected thyroid problems, diabetes, anaemia, hormone difficulties, such as low testosterone, indeed a range of physical problems.

Physical illness itself can be a source of depression. Indeed, anything that creates pain or disrupts our capacity to live a meaningful and active life can affect our mood. Sexual difficulties and the shame of talking about them can be depressing for both men and women, contributing to unhappiness in their partnerships. They can contribute to the fear of forming intimate relationships and hence contribute to loneliness. Depression has been discussed in different ways in different cultures and at different historic periods. This reflects not only different ways of understanding depression, but also that people expressed their suffering in different ways according to culture and context. Today we have a growing problem of self-harming, particularly in the younger generations, whereas 200 years ago young people rarely cut or burned themselves.

The fact of the matter is that historically human life has often been harsh and a struggle. Fifty per cent of all Romans, for example, died before the age of 10 because diseases were so prevalent and conditions so harsh. We live in a world where we all want to be happy and indeed we expect to be happy, and yet happiness requires certain conditions for it to flourish – it is not a naturally given state of mind. Happiness will not flourish in conditions of social conflict, abuse, violence, neglect, and where we are surrounded constantly by signals overstimulating us and confronting us with how much better and how much more others have than we do. Research has shown that it is not just absolute poverty that is the problem – it is relative poverty. The greater the disparities between the rich and poor, the more mental health problems societies have.

Rates of postnatal depression are much lower in cultures where women are well integrated into kin networks. In wealthier countries we live in a very competitive society where we are constantly being directed to self-monitor and judge ourselves in the sense: 'I'm not good enough; I'm not up to this.' It is reported that when the Dalai Lama first came to the West, he could not understand how people could dislike themselves and be so self-critical. Having a hostile relationship with oneself is now known to be highly associated with depression vulnerability. Questions arise as to how do people acquire such hostile and critical views of themselves? What can also sit underneath some of our depression is not just anger and disappointment in the self but about the way life is. Many depressed people can be frightened of their anger, worried about expressing it, risking a counter attack or rejection, and upset if they express it to their children. When all you really want is to feel connected, valued, and loved, it's tough to have to deal with these feelings.

Depression is increasing as part of the modern age but we are not evolving genes for depression, we are cultivating lifestyles to breed it. We are living increasingly in an age where we are reduced to objects of competition, despite the extraordinary outpouring of compassion and mutual support generated by Covid-19. It is the role of psychologists to highlight that we are a highly social interdependent species. From the day we are born to the day we die, the kindness and compassion of others will have a huge impact on the quality of our lives – even changing the way our genes work (what biologists call gene expression: epigenetics). Consider that even at a conservative estimate, 5 per cent of us are depressed, then for every million people

we have 50,000 who are depressed. In a country the size of the UK we are talking over 3 million people. We're not going to tackle that with individual therapy solutions. Countless studies have shown that the more connected and supported we feel in our communities, the lower the levels of distress. Hence building compassionate and supportive communities would be a major target for intervention and prevention.

Psychologists have a major role in helping people understand what they are caught up in and to begin to soften the chains of self-criticism, self-blame and shame. There is increasing evidence that a compassionate focus to ourselves and others has many mental and health benefits. Psychological interventions need to be more social and contextual, focusing more on prosociality rather than just rationality. Our physiologies are co-regulated through our relationships.

In this document the British Psychological Society has brought together important insights into what depression is, the common causes for it and what we can do. Understanding these biopsychosocial dimensions of depression is the biggest challenge of the next decades because the solutions to our mental health problems and the promotion of wellbeing anfd flourishing are both individual but also collective and relational. The British Psychological Society offers important blueprints for this moving forward on many fronts – from diets and exercise to epigenetics, from personal therapies and mind training practices, to social and collective movements. There is much to inspire us here.

# Executive summary

# Executive summary

## A PSYCHOLOGICAL APPROACH TO DEPRESSION

Depression is a common human experience that can be life-threatening. It deserves to be taken seriously and needs a compassionate response. Everyone's experience is slightly different, as are the reasons for it. This report particularly emphasises the psychological aspects of depression, together with ideas about what can help both on an individual level and in terms of reducing the number of people affected. The report is primarily focused on the experience of depression in adults, although some factors will also be relevant for children, and childhood factors are often important in why people become depressed later in life.

## EXPERIENCE OR ILLNESS?

This report argues that depression is best thought of as an **experience**, or a set of experiences, **rather than as a disease**. The experience we call depression is a form of distress. The depth of distress itself, as well as the contributing events and circumstances, can be life-changing, and even life-threatening. However, calling it an illness is only one way of thinking about it, with advantages and disadvantages. For many people, depression is unlikely to be the result of an underlying biological disease process or chemical imbalance in the brain and nervous system. Even if there are changes in the brain when people are depressed these are often consequences not primary causes. After all, all mental states have physiological and biochemical elements. Even when we fall in love things change in our brain. The discovery of physical changes in depression tells us nothing about causality or even the best ways for helping. Whilst of course our brains are involved in all experiences, the reasons for depression are usually complex and include the events and circumstances of people's lives and the ways they can respond to them.

## LIFE EVENTS AND CIRCUMSTANCES

Often, the experience of depression is related to the **events and circumstances** of a person's life, both in the past and the present, together with the meaning those events have for them. The brain plays a role too, as it does in all experiences. Different people and cultures understand and describe these experiences in different ways. However, there are recognisable common themes, including hopelessness, loss and threats to self-esteem. We also know that depression is linked to feeling out of control, helpless, trapped or defeated in certain life situations when someone does not know how to get out of them or who to turn to. It is very important to recognise that it's not the person's fault when they feel this way.

Life circumstances are massively important in understanding why people become depressed. These include life events, especially events involving loss of some kind, but also ongoing threats such as poverty, inequity, uncertainty and for many, oppression. Depression is often associated with a lack of a close confidant and difficulties in relationships. The frequent assumption that 'mental illnesses' have internal or biological causes risks distracting attention from the effects of people's life circumstances. We need to bear this in mind when we describe and explain these experiences, and when we support others who are depressed. Life circumstances and the availability of options and resources are central to reducing and preventing depression.

## SOCIAL INEQUALITIES

There are inter-connections between health, mental health and unequal societies. Individuals and communities who face multiple deprivations often have high levels of stress, isolation and depression. Therefore, progress in reducing income and social inequalities (e.g. reducing the gender and ethnicity pay gaps, increasing the early detection of people's difficulties and referring on to services and support for the rights and needs of all people with 'protected characteristics' under the Equality Act) is likely to have a positive impact on wellbeing and on the prevention of depression.

## PSYCHOLOGICALLY HEALTHY ENVIRONMENTS

Environments which promote wellbeing are important too. We need more of these in every aspect of life: employment, housing, transport and education. Access to green spaces and community resources also contribute to psychological health.

## RELATIONSHIPS

When people experience depression, their relationships are often affected. Two things stand out. Firstly, the quality of the relationships the person has with themselves, for example how self-critical or compassionate they are towards themselves. Second is the quality of relationships the person has with others, whether they experience support and connectedness or the opposite. Stressful or abusive relationships can contribute to becoming depressed, but once a person is depressed, any or all of their relationships can suffer because they have less capacity to appreciate and cope with other people.

## HELPFUL RESPONSES AND THERAPIES

Overcoming depression can sometimes be a difficult and slow process. Nevertheless, there are **many things which can help**. Different things help different people. Often practical things are central such as basic self-care, including eating and sleeping well, as well as help to address the issues that led to the depression or that are keeping it going, physical exercise or therapies of various kinds. Psychological therapies help many people. Depression and loneliness often go hand in hand, so finding ways to connect or reconnect with our friends, families and communities can be key.

## PERSONAL MEANING

We all make sense of the things that happen to us, and the way we do this is often shaped by our experiences in childhood and the culture and society that surrounds us. An event that is trivial or even benign for one person may be very depressing for another, because of what it means to that person. This is one of the reasons that help and support from services needs to be guided by a personal, collaboratively drawn up **formulation.**

## COLLABORATIVE FORMULATIONS

People experience depression for different reasons, and for different combinations of reasons. There is no one simple explanation that applies in all cases, but we do know a lot about the different factors that can play a role. The most helpful thing that professionals can do is usually to sit down with each person and try and work out the particular things that appear to be playing a role for them and to do this in a culturally sensitive way. Crucial to this process is that the depressed person feels that the clinician is really listening to, accepting of, and interested in him or her.

We recommend that all care and treatment within mental health services is guided by individual formulations, developed and refined over time by the professional/s and the person concerned working together. A formulation is different from diagnosis – it is a joint effort between a service user and a healthcare professional to summarise their difficulties, to explain why they may be happening and make sense of them, and so to suggest what might help.[2]

# Part 1: Depression –
# A human experience

# Part 1: Depression – A human experience

Sometimes, just waking up in the mornings and getting out of bed feels like the hardest task in the world... I used to wake up in the mornings and literally feel sick as soon as I awoke. I'd feel a surge of dread and nausea right in the pit of my stomach and I just wanted to throw the duvet over my head and not have to face the outside world.

**Jonny Benjamin**

## KEY POINTS

Each person's experience of depression is different.

Persistent depression is a significant problem for many people, and for our society.

There is a debate about what we mean by depression. Calling depression an illness is only one way of thinking about it, with advantages and disadvantages.

The experience of depression lies on a continuum – a continuous line from not at all depressed to very depressed, and it changes constantly – therefore it becomes less helpful to think of either 'having' or 'not having' depression.

Our cultural and social background influences the way we experience, understand and talk about depression.

# WHAT DOES IT MEAN TO EXPERIENCE DEPRESSION?

Sometimes people can experience an extended period of low mood that, while it lasts, can profoundly affect their everyday lives, relationships, and sense of purpose and meaning. Everyone's experience is different, but it might include:

feelings of misery and worthlessness

a sense of emptiness and numbness

feelings of shame or dread

physical and mental lethargy and exhaustion

disturbed sleep

increased or decreased appetite

loneliness, isolation and lack of connection

wanting to be on our own, isolating ourselves

changes in everyday routines and activities

finding it difficult to make everyday decisions

fear

anger

frustration, desperation and a sense of meaninglessness

feeling trapped

suicidal thoughts

feeling that there is no hope for the future.

# A SIGNIFICANT PROBLEM IN OUR SOCIETY

The experience of depression is very common and the World Health Organization has described depression as the commonest of all health problems.[3] At any one time, over 300 million people around the world are experiencing mood that is so low that they would meet formal criteria for a 'diagnosis of depression'.[4] More than 80 per cent of these people live in low- and middle-income countries although recorded rates are generally higher in high income countries (meaning that people are more likely to receive a diagnosis of depression in high income countries).[5]

At any one time between 4 per cent and 10 per cent of us, including children,[6,7] are experiencing depression serious enough to affect our work, study or personal lives. It is

hard to know how much to rely on global and national estimates given the different ways depression is described and categorised across different groups and populations. Nevertheless, it is clear that the experiences we call depression are very common.

**Depression**
Like the deepest, darkest pit. Like a tunnel without an end.
Darkness surrounding you, Despair enfolding you,
Death overwhelming you.

**LR**

# FEELING SUICIDAL

For some people, the experience of depression, or the circumstances that led to depression, are so intolerable that they contemplate ending their lives. As many as 1 in 10 people receiving help from their GP for depression may attempt suicide over a five-year period.[8,9] After a death it is not always possible to know for sure that the person meant to take their own life, and coroners tend to avoid recording a suicide if there is any doubt. Even so, the official UK population suicide rate is about 1 in 10,000, which equates to around 6,000 people each year.[10] Across the UK, the suicide rate is three times higher in men than in women. There are some variations across the four nations, though rates of male suicide were declining until recently. In Scotland, the general reduction in suicides seems to be driven by fewer suicides amongst women although suicide amongst young men in Scotland is increasing. Age-specific suicide rates increase with age from 10 to 14 year-olds through to 40 to 54 year-olds; rates then fall until the age group 70 to 74 year-olds before increasing again for older age groups.[11] The same UK official figures indicate the suicide rate for middle-aged men, notably those aged 45 to 49 is particularly high. Middle-aged men are more likely to be affected by economic adversity, difficulties with alcoholism and isolation; furthermore, this group are less inclined to seek help.[12] For women, the highest suicide rate is from the age of 50 to 54. Suicide rates increase from ages 80 years and over and men in this age group are about four times more likely to die by suicide than women. Many factors contribute to this widely seen phenomenon around the world such as the deterioration of mental and physical health, bereavement, social isolation and poverty.[13]

In Part 4 of this report, there is a section that covers what to do in a time of crisis, and the resources section lists organisations that give support (see p.68 and p.77).

> When I have low mood it can last as long as between a couple of weeks to two years, with six months average. I feel desperate, 'Emotional Death'. I am frightened of the future, I fear life and welcome death. I have attempted suicide several times since I have no hope and fear the future, since I don't think I will ever get better.
>
> **Belle**

> There is a point where it becomes what we call an illness – we don't function properly. The problem lies… in what we attach to the idea of illness. If the concept of illness was extended from biology to include our emotional/spiritual/thinking and meaning-making faculties, we would have an holistic approach which would offer more.
>
> **Laura**

There is a vigorous debate about whether it is meaningful or useful to think of depression as a mental illness. This is an important debate because the different ways of understanding depression have broad-reaching implications for our society and for how we can best offer help to those affected.

People often assume that mental illnesses 'exist' in the same way that broken bones exist, and that there are independent tests for them such as blood tests or scans. However, this is not the case for mental health problems.[14] While popular, the idea that depression is caused by a chemical imbalance or other problem in the brain is only one theory with little hard evidence to support it.[15,16,17]

Another idea is that, rather than being an experience thrust upon us by biology, depression, like other emotions, is often an understandable human response to the world around us that involves complex evaluations of events.[18]

Nevertheless, depression can be very debilitating, and so thinking of it as an illness in our current social context can have some advantages. It gives us a way of talking about suffering and a framework for receiving help: time off work with sick pay or benefits if needed, for example, and access to services.

> When I eventually plucked up courage to go to the student counsellor to talk about my problems, the university authorities granted me the opportunity to repeat a year 'because you have been ill'. At first that sounded like a strange way to describe my trials and tribulations but in some ways, it was accurate, since I was suffering a lot, and so were my studies. It was reassuring to have a diagnosis of depression at the time. In my naivety, I assumed that it explained why I was in a mess, as if there were an illness that I had somehow caught and it was nothing to do with difficult stuff in my life – much easier just to think, OK, it's an illness that has got hold of me, and the doctors will sort it out. As others seemed to find my situation as baffling as I did, it was easiest all round just to be able to say, 'I've got depression'. The diagnosis also went with hope of getting help and support.
>
> **Annie**

I think I prefer my illness having a name because it makes me feel less lonely, and I know that there are other people experiencing my kind of misery. And that people live through my illness and make a meaningful existence with it. But I also have to be careful not to adopt the sick role, since I know I would just give up if I did that.

**Karin Falk**

## DEPRESSION ON A CONTINUUM

Another common assumption is that there is a straightforward dividing line between 'mental health' and 'mental illness', between normality and abnormality. We often talk as if depression is either present or absent. But it may be more helpful to think in terms of a continuum – a continuous line from very depressed to not at all depressed.

Mood can also change from moment to moment and over the course of a day. Even in the darkest depression there can be lighter moments.[19]

Depression is so fluid. It can change from hour to hour, day to day and week to week and so on.

**Member of Survivors of Depression in Transition (SODIT) group**

Uncertainty of mood, for example fine in the morning not good in the afternoon. Day to day or even hour by hour.

**Kerry**

Whilst we all share a common humanity and can empathise with each other's experiences, it is also the case that, as with all human experiences, no one person's problems, or ways of coping with them, are the same as anyone else's. Depression is an individual experience: our circumstances vary, and we each respond differently to them.

Some people feel overwhelmed by sorrow, grief, anger or exhaustion. Some are unable to feel any pleasure or joy in the normal things of life – which is sometimes called 'anhedonia'.

Some people experience intrusive thoughts that can be distressing and distracting. Some feel better later in the day, while others feel low all day.[20] Some have thoughts and feelings of hopelessness about the future[21] or a feeling of being stuck or trapped.[22] Some feel that they are bad and deserve to be punished. Some find it hard to remember things or concentrate.[23] Sometimes people may find themselves 'ruminating': going over and over the same ground, for example constantly asking themselves why they have been so stupid or bad, or why they have messed up their lives.[24]

Some people feel depressed for many years or repeatedly. Others may have ups and downs but only ever have one experience of being so depressed that it is difficult to function.

People also express their feelings in different ways. For example, younger people may feel tearful or angry and not want to see their friends, whereas older people may experience pain, and sleep problems and report physical rather than emotional problems such as faintness or dizziness.[25,26] One study suggests that women experience depression more in the form of feeling stressed, irritable, losing sleep and losing interest in things they would normally enjoy, whereas men are more likely to get angry and aggressive, misuse substances and take other sorts of risks.[27] However, these are broad generalisations; we are all different. Our particular circumstances also play a role – for example a loss may be linked to sadness whereas being bullied may link to closing down and feeling fearful.

> There were days when I struggled with excruciating bouts of self-attacking thoughts and emotions. Often I was so distracted that it was hard to string words together. It was exhausting.
>
> **Annie**

> Some days it feels like walls are closing in on me, so I have to walk out and walk for hours before I can go back home, whereas some days I don't leave the house at all.
>
> **Kerry**

## LANGUAGE AND CULTURE

The way that we think and talk about mental and emotional suffering varies among cultures.[28] Depending on our cultural environment, it might be more usual to describe emotional suffering in terms of physical pain, fatigue, a heavy heart, or feeling depressed.[29,30,31,32] Similarly, our cultural background may influence the way we, or those around us, make sense of what we do and say. Cultural attitudes to depression may mean that some people do not identify their difficulties or access support when needed.

## NAMES FOR DEPRESSION WE MAY EXPERIENCE AT PARTICULAR TIMES

Health professionals and researchers sometimes classify depression by the time or context when it occurs. For example, depression during pregnancy can be called 'antenatal depression' and after the birth of a baby 'postnatal depression'. Some people tend to experience depression in winter or when light levels are low, when it might be called 'seasonal affective disorder' (SAD).[33] These labels don't represent different 'types' of depression. They are labels for depression at different times when our experiences may be particularly difficult. This could be for physical, social or psychological reasons – or a combination of these.

## WHEN PERIODS OF DEPRESSION ALTERNATE WITH ELATION

Some people have periods of low mood but also periods of elation, which if they are intense, health professionals sometimes call 'mania' or 'hypomania'. The tendency to experience extremes of mood can also be referred to as 'bipolar disorder'. People who are very elated ('on a high') often feel great and have lots of energy, racing thoughts and little need for sleep. Some people find that they are more creative than usual during these periods of heightened energy.[34] However, they may also feel restless and irritable and find it difficult to focus on tasks. People may end up doing things they later regret, like going on a spending spree and running up debts. For a more in-depth discussion of these experiences, see the British Psychological Society's public information report *Understanding Bipolar Disorder*.[35]

## WHEN DEPRESSION INCLUDES PSYCHOTIC EXPERIENCES

People who are depressed – especially if they are severely depressed – may also hear, see, smell, taste or feel things that others don't, or start fearing or believing that people want to harm them.[36,37] This can be frightening or distressing, both for the person experiencing it and for those around them. These may be called psychotic experiences or psychosis and may lead to a diagnosis of 'psychotic depression'. As in other cases, these experiences can be caused by trauma, sleep deprivation, physical illness and/or use of street drugs or too much alcohol.[38] For more information on these experiences, see the British Psychological Society's public information report *Understanding Psychosis*.[39]

# Part 2: Why do we become depressed?

# Part 2: Why do we become depressed?

> If you live a long life and get to the end of it without ever once having felt crushingly depressed, then you probably haven't been paying attention.
>
> **Duncan Macmillan[40]**

## KEY POINTS

Depression is a common human experience which happens for a variety of reasons.

It is often related at least in part to the events and circumstances of our lives and the meaning we make of them, which means depression can be explained and understood.

Life events that can lead to depression include threat, oppression or loss, in childhood or adulthood or both.

We live in an increasingly 'depressogenic' society (i.e. one that can lead to or maintain depression) characterised by inequality, isolation, social comparison and, for many, oppression.

# THE DEBATE ABOUT CAUSES

The search for causes has often focused on genetics and on aspects of brain functioning.[41] Psychologists have also looked at the way that people interpret information and their 'thinking styles'. However, professionals are increasingly acknowledging that the primary reasons for depression often lie in the events and circumstances of our lives. There is no 'one size fits all' explanation. Different combinations of causes are likely to be relevant for different people, and to interact with each other.

People who have experienced depression hold a variety of views about the nature and causes of their difficulties. The reasons we become depressed are usually complex. Since no one professional is in a position to know for sure exactly which elements combined to cause problems for a particular person, it is crucial to respect all views.

Like other human experiences, the experience of depression involves thoughts, emotions and behaviours (things we do). We can look at depression in terms of its brain chemistry (which neurotransmitters might be involved, for instance), its psychology (for example, the effect of depressed mood on the way we think) or its social context (what has happened to make us depressed). All human experiences involve the brain, but this is just as much the case for experiences such as happiness or love as it is for depression or any of the experiences we call 'mental health problems'.

> I can still remember the moment depression hit me and the event that triggered it. Those issues are now resolved so why do I still have depression?
>
> **Member of Survivors of Depression in Transition (SODIT) group**

# OUT OF THE BLUE

Although depression often follows major life events,[42] this is not true for everyone. Sometimes it can seem that depression comes out of the blue.[43] It can feel as if there is no explanation for depression but that it has just happened. Although it's tempting to assume, in these circumstances, that there is a biological cause, it's also possible that there is no single 'cause' but rather vicious circles that are keeping the person's mood low. In these circumstances it can feel as if there is no way to make sense of the way they are feeling; they just are that way and can feel very stuck. It's easy in this situation to stop doing things that might help – physical activity, purposeful work, meeting with loved ones or friends.

Similarly, when people are depressed, it's harder to stay optimistic, to think of themselves in a positive way, or to 'bounce back' after disappointments.

Sometimes the causes of distress are 'invisible' due to strongly held beliefs that we or those around us, or society holds. An example is the assumption that having certain material things, or being married, or having just had a baby means you must be happy. Things are never as simple as this, and any number of things can make us miserable at times when we might feel we 'should' be happy.

# LIFE EXPERIENCES

Many life events and circumstances can lead to depression, particularly ones involving threat or loss.[44,45] It is common, natural and understandable to feel low and hopeless if faced with a situation of ongoing threat in which we have little control, for example a life-threatening illness, discrimination, financial problems, violence in a relationship, exploitation, bullying or homelessness.

Experiences involving loss, for example bereavement, migration, fertility difficulties, loss of religious faith, betrayal, redundancy, retirement, divorce, enforced immobility due to illness or disability, failing at something significant to us, or losing status in our community, can also lead to depression. This is particularly the case if people don't have supportive friends or family to whom they can turn. Having said this, some people may experience threat or loss and **not** become depressed. We are all different and our life experiences and circumstances affect us in different ways. Brown and Harris's 'Camberwell Study' (see the box below), was one of the first to demonstrate the profound effects of life circumstances.

## The Camberwell Study

In the 1970s, researchers George Brown and Tirril Harris[46] carried out extensive research in South London looking at the link between people's circumstances and their mental health. They looked at women in particular and found that they were more likely to become depressed if they had experienced a particular life event, namely losing their mother in early life, and if they were in particular life circumstances, namely having three or more young children at home and not being in paid work.

The study also found that people were more likely to experience depression if, in addition to these difficult life circumstances, something happened that affected their role or standing within their community, or the way they saw themselves. So, for example, if her son got into trouble with the law, a woman might lose the sense that she was a good mother. The study reported that support from friends and family or having someone to confide in made a big difference, particularly at a time of crisis.

Other researchers[47] have built on the Camberwell study, suggesting that our idea of who we are – our 'sense of self' – is crucial for psychological health. Redundancy, for example, can affect both our social roles and our sense of self. As well as enabling us to pay the bills, going to work every day can give us a sense of purpose and meaning, of being someone with something to offer, and of belonging to a team.[48] This may be one of the reasons why unemployment is associated with depression, although so are exploitative working conditions.[49,50]

Researchers have also looked at other events or circumstances that may lead to depression, discussed next.

Sometimes it can really help me if I write down 'reasons to be unhappy just now'. That might seem like a recipe for feeling bad, but if I'm **already** feeling bad and I just can't put my finger on why, or it keeps slipping away, sometimes making a list can make me feel a bit better. I'm not just being miserable to annoy someone. Sometimes it's important to just allow yourself to say, 'Yes, OK, this is actually a bit stressful, a bit difficult, and of course it's affecting the way I feel.' Sometimes then you can also do something about it, or you can tell someone close to you that it's difficult when they may not have realised.

**Annie**

## CHILDHOOD EXPERIENCES

A major study conducted in America over several years[51] demonstrated that people who have difficult experiences in childhood are more likely to experience physical and mental health problems as adults (see the box below). The study's findings are significant and there have been more than 50 scientific articles and more than 100 conferences and workshops discussing its implications.

**The adverse childhood experiences (or ACEs) study**

The 'adverse childhood experiences' (or ACEs) found to be associated with later problems include:

- Physical abuse

- Sexual abuse

- Emotional abuse

- Physical neglect

- Witnessing violence towards one's mother

- Substance abuse in the household

- Serious mental health problems in the household

- Parental separation or divorce

- Imprisonment of household member

The more of these a person experiences as a child, the more likely they are to experience depression later in life.[52,53,54,55] One recent study has shown that depression due to trauma is also apparent in children.[56]

Other studies have shown that people who suffer sexual abuse as children are more likely than others to experience depression as adults and may experience it more frequently and for longer periods.[57,58] This is particularly the case for those who have been abused by more than one person, or have suffered emotional or physical abuse as well.[59,60] Those who have been sexually abused in childhood are also more likely to have suicidal feelings or to harm themselves later in life. Women who have survived sexual abuse in childhood are 20 times, and men 14 times more likely than others to consider suicide.[61,62,63] The numbers are even higher for people who have also experienced other kinds of neglect or abuse as children.

> Unsupported trauma in early years had a huge effect on my adult life. I only experienced depression in later life due to a trigger which then fed into childhood experiences. It took many years to get to grips with.
>
> **Member of Survivors of Depression in Transition (SODIT) group**

## ABUSE AND BULLYING

People who were abused, neglected or bullied as children are more likely than others to experience depression (and also anxiety) as adults.[64] We know that young people who are bullied often experience depression[65] and that it is generally harmful to mental health.[66,67] Bullying can be psychological as well as physical, and may be harder to escape nowadays as it can also occur online.[68] The inability to escape bullying can lead to feelings of helplessness and hopelessness, and people sometimes blame themselves for supposed weakness.[69,70] Of course, bullying happens to adults too and can be by our intimate partners or spouses,[71,72] by our friends, family, employer or work colleagues.[73,74]

## STRESSES ON PARENTS

The link between depression and being a parent is complex. There can be many positive aspects to parenthood. However, it can also be difficult. Families may be trapped by conditions of social deprivation and health inequalities.[75,76] Factors like high rents, high property prices and low pay can leave families trapped in situations of hardship.

The combined problems of isolation, lack of freedom and economic inequality affect many parents and therefore their families and have been particularly prevalent during 'austerity'. These factors can have a strong negative effect on parents' mental health and make them more likely to experience depression.[77] This can be very significant for many parents, particularly women who are often in caring roles in families. Children leaving home as adults can also be stressful for parents for many different reasons. Older parents may also have the stress of continuing to financially support adult children.

## THE IMPACT OF AUSTERITY

The political environment in the UK in recent years, with its focus on austerity policies has inflicted great misery on many with damaging psychological costs. A United Nations report[78] highlighted that about a fifth of the UK population now lives in relative poverty and 1.5 million are destitute and unable to afford basic essentials. Another recent review[79] concluded that funding cuts to public services have been 'regressive and inequitable', suggesting that these financial decisions have 'harmed health and contributed to widening health inequalities.' Austerity policies can have negative psychological effects such as increases in humiliation and shame, fear and distrust, instability and insecurity, isolation and loneliness, and being trapped and powerless.[80] Sometimes, the effects on people's mental health are profound. For example, if someone experiences both a significant loss and prolonged humiliation, they are three times more likely than average to be diagnosed with clinical depression.[81] Unemployment is damaging for mental health, but so is job insecurity.[82,83,84]

## SOCIAL DISADVANTAGE

There is a clear link between depression and social disadvantage:[85] poverty, poor housing, stressful or low-status jobs, missing out on formal qualifications, living in crowded city areas, or having to move home frequently.[86,87,88,89,90,91] Spending time in secure accommodation or in care[92] or in prison[93] also makes it more likely that someone will experience depression.

> My muscles felt so weak... my hips, my legs, everywhere. I could've sat in that sofa and not got out...ever.
>
> **Kay**

## PHYSICAL ILLNESS

People with ongoing health problems such as diabetes, cancer and heart disease often experience depression.[94,95] This is probably largely because of the impact on quality of life,[96] but it can also be related to being dependent on others[97] or in some cases to prejudice and discrimination. As people age they can be more susceptible to various health conditions so age is a risk factor for various physical illnesses and consequently depression. Given the ACEs study (mentioned earlier), it is also possible that some physical illnesses and depression have the same long-term cause, that is, stressful childhood events and circumstances.

## GENDER

Many more women than men receive a diagnosis of 'depressive disorder'.[98] There are a number of possible reasons for this. It may be in part because of the way we define depression: the criteria emphasise sadness and tearfulness. In many cultures, it is more acceptable for women to show their distress by crying, while men often express their emotions through anger or aggression and could therefore be less likely to see themselves, or be seen by others, as depressed.[99]

Women and girls also have a different experience of life from men and boys. For example, they are more likely to experience certain types of trauma such as domestic or sexual abuse.[100] These kinds of experiences can have a profound impact on our mental health; women who experienced abuse as children, or whose intimate partners are violent to them, are much more likely than others to experience depression.[101,102,103,104] Approximately half of women referred to mental health services may have suffered sexual abuse in childhood.[105]

In addition, women often carry more care responsibilities, are less valued than men within society, and have to contend with restrictive and oppressive expectations. Women are also more likely than men to be on low wages, and generally have less power and autonomy.[106] All these things may contribute to higher rates of depression.[107,108]

That said, the apparently lower rates of depression in men could be a result of them expressing their feelings differently or being less likely to ask for help. Compared with women, men are less likely to go to their GP or seek support from family or friends and are more likely to use alcohol and drugs to attempt to manage their distress.[109]

## MARGINALISATION

In general, being part of a group makes us less likely to experience depression.[110] However, if the group is a marginalised one, being a member of it can also expose us to prejudice and discrimination. People from ethnic minority backgrounds have an increased likelihood of experiencing depression.[111] So do people of diverse sexuality: that is, who are, for example, lesbian, gay, bisexual or transgender.[112] Women from ethnic minority backgrounds may experience the double disadvantage of both gender and racial discrimination.[113] People with physical or learning disabilities are more likely than others to experience depression,[114,115] as are older people,[116] possibly due to the potential of increasing disability and isolation as we age.

Understanding depression

> Just before my 21st birthday, I had a breakdown... I had depression, and part of that depression was from being so scared, so terrified of coming out. I got taken into hospital, and I stayed there for 6 weeks and while I was there I finally said the words that I dreaded, and each time I said to people that I was gay it was kind of like a weight lifting off my shoulders each time... and I felt such a relief.
>
> **Jonny Benjamin**

### PREJUDICE AND DISCRIMINATION

Negative attitudes in society can foster subtle or even blatant aggression, ostracism and discrimination.[117] All of this can be very damaging to people's mental wellbeing[118] and can lead to depression.[119] A large research study on the life experiences of people from minority ethnic backgrounds suggests that people who have experienced discrimination are more likely than others to experience depression.[120] Our sense of self comes partly from how we fit into the roles that society has created. We tend to follow 'scripts' or 'social actions'[121] which make it hard for us to see that society's current ideas about a whole range of issues – for example poverty or mental health – are not necessarily the most helpful for everyone, but just how we happen to think about things in a particular culture at a particular time. An example is the idea that people are largely responsible for their own misfortune. Some of these ideas can be based on ignorance, prejudice or discrimination. On a smaller scale, this can also happen with ideas that are passed down in families. This can make it hard for us to question them – the status quo becomes seen as the only possible way of organising and understanding things.[122] It is also possible for people to internalise prejudice and feel bad about who they are.[123]

### MIGRATION

Although migration can enrich our lives with positive experiences and opportunities, it can also be very stressful. People who have migrated to a new country may face racism and other forms of discrimination and might also have to contend with structural challenges – such as not being eligible for employment that matches their skills – and economic inequality.[124] Living in a new place may be a positive decision for many, but for others this might not be a choice but a necessity, as people are forced to move for political or economic reasons. Underlying all of this is the possibility that those of us who have left behind family, friends and culture, for any reason, may experience deep feelings of loss related to this significant change. Even if we have lived in the country that we migrated to for many years, we can be at a higher risk of depression than other people if we experience highly stressful life events.[125]

> As a child, I suffered a bereavement, and loss of my home, school, country, way of life.
>
> **Belle**

## CLIMATE CHANGE

There is growing awareness of a causal link between climate change and mental health issues. This happens both as a result of the many current and future environmental changes and stressors which increase social inequalities, trauma and social unrest,[126] and on a personal level of anxiety, grief and mourning.[127]

> Everything was taken away – I've spent a lifetime to put it back.
>
> KL

# HOW OUR EXPERIENCES CAN AFFECT US

Both early experiences and current circumstances can lead to depression.

## THE IMPORTANCE OF EARLY RELATIONSHIPS

The bond that children develop with their parents or primary caregivers plays a vital function in laying the groundwork for forming other relationships as we grow up.[128] If caregiving is sensitive and responsive, we develop the ability to become 'securely attached' to the caregiver. On the other hand, if early experiences were less good, we can develop 'insecure' attachments.[129] This can happen when those we depend on are struggling with overwhelming circumstances or with their own distress or illness, or if they are neglectful or even violent towards us. However, even if we had difficult early relationships, if there was at least one person we could trust at some time when we were growing up – a friend or family member for example, a youth worker or perhaps a therapist – this can help us become more trusting of others.[130,131]

The attachment style we develop can influence our later relationships, both with others and ourselves. If we had insecure attachments, we may find it difficult to form close trusting relationships and this can mean we feel lonely and alone with the inevitable emotional distresses we face in life. Difficult early attachments can also replay in conflicted current relationships. This can mean we are more likely to experience depression or other mental health difficulties.

## HOW SOME EXPERIENCES CAN AFFECT THE WAY WE SEE THE WORLD

Painful experiences in childhood affect our developing view of ourselves, of the world and of other people.[132] If we experience bullying or repeated criticism, say, or perhaps the death of a parent, this will affect our beliefs, our ways of thinking and the ways we respond to events in later life.[133] For example, if we are constantly criticised, we may come to see ourselves as bad and others as attacking. These ways of seeing the world are sometimes called 'schemas'.[134] Our schemas influence how we make sense of things and how we judge ourselves, our situation and other people. While we are growing up, they can be helpful in making sense of our situation and guiding our actions. However, they can be hard to shift as our situation changes over time, and sometimes particular schemas can end up being unhelpful and adding to our distress. For example, someone might have taken on impossible standards of perfection or achievement from their family, who may have focused on success rather than effort. Such a focus can demoralise, as it encourages a fixed mindset:[135] the belief that we are either good or poor at something, for instance, as opposed to being in a constant state of learning and personal growth. Then when we encounter a setback, we may feel that we have failed, because it was about who we are, rather than a step along a road from which we can learn. This sense of failure can contribute to depression.

> There were two different kinds of family sayings about me as a child: One was along the lines of 'She's a clever clogs and one day she'll be the next [major social position]' and 'She's a horrid creature, stupid, a nuisance, in the way, etc., etc.' When I was succeeding, things were sort of OK. When I started failing, I felt I had let everyone down. They thought I was going to do amazing things, and now it was all going to pieces. I was the horrid creature I had always been: just a nuisance.
>
> **Annie**

## HOW LIFE AFFECTS OUR GENES

People used to think that the genes you were born with stayed the same throughout life, so people were essentially genetically destined to think or behave in certain ways. More recently, however, it has been discovered that, while our genes remain the same and are passed on to our children, different genes can be 'switched on' or 'off' as a result of things that happen in our lives. The study of this is called epigenetics.[136] This means that the genes we inherit from our parents are not the whole explanation of our current biological make-up.

### EVOLUTIONARY ADAPTATIONS

Evolution has shaped the many genetic variations among people, and in general it is a positive force, giving us a host of capacities to cope with our environment.[137] For instance, the capacity to react to another person's anger by becoming fearful or submissive can save our lives, so evolution has ensured that these reactions continue.[138] Distress calls from young animals separated from their mothers may reunite them, but if they are alone for a long time, the young animals tend to become passive, quiet and motionless; that way they are less likely to be noticed by a predator and they preserve energy.[139] The modern effect of these evolutionary adaptations is that if we receive poor care in childhood, we are more likely to react passively to dangers and defeats as adults which can make us more likely to experience depression.[140]

## HOW OUR BODIES REACT TO STRESS OR SAFETY

Our basic biological systems affect our emotions and how we behave. We have an in-built mechanism for avoiding threats and another for seeking things we find rewarding.[141] These mechanisms can be affected by the things that happen to us. For example, a childhood full of abuse and danger might lead us to focus mainly on avoiding threats and remaining alert to danger. This would cause stress for the body which is associated with the release of the hormone cortisol. In the short term this prepares the body for action and helps with reactions to threatening situations. When people experience severe or on-going stress, their brain's stress response system may constantly be in a state of 'high alert'.[142] This might make us prone to anxiety later in life, frequently thinking about what we should be doing to avoid something bad happening.

Similarly, a childhood lacking in rewards might lead us to feel powerless, that nothing we do will work. This can make us pessimistic and prone to depression.

Another in-built need for humans is to feel close to others. This is part of our social nature and can be called the affiliative (closeness to others) system.[143] It enables us to feel soothed, safe and content. In this state, it is easier for us to put ourselves in someone else's shoes – to have empathy and to 'mentalise' (understand our own and other people's feelings and needs).[144] The ability to have compassion for ourselves and others is vital to our general health and wellbeing and that of those around us.

## STRESS AND INFLAMMATION

Emerging evidence suggests that ongoing stress, such as physical or psychological abuse in childhood[145] or long-term isolation, can lead to over-activity of the immune system, which in turn leads to inflammation[146]. Inflammation is the body's usual response to injury or infection, and it can make us feel fatigued and lower our appetite. In some cases, this might contribute to depression[147] and, in theory, anti-inflammatory medication could help. However, research into this is in its early stages.[148] Generally, it seems sensible to focus on reducing sources of prolonged stress rather than focusing on counteracting its effects with drugs.

## BRAIN CHEMICALS (NEUROTRANSMITTERS)

Neurotransmitters are chemical messengers in our brain and central nervous system. Many people assume that depression is caused by an imbalance of these chemicals. For obvious reasons, it is in pharmaceutical companies' interests to promote this idea. One company's website states that 'Clinical depression... is a serious medical condition... believed to be caused by an imbalance of chemicals, called neurotransmitters.'[149] Although often reported uncritically by the media, this view is not currently supported by the evidence.[150,151,152]

Many neurological and biochemical pathways in the brain are likely to be involved in experiences such as low mood or suicidal thoughts. However, as we discussed earlier, this is also the case for all other human experiences. Our brain chemistry is different when we are happy, or in love, bored, irritated or sad, or when we are looking at a face or a tree. The undoubted existence of biological aspects to all human experiences, including low mood and despair, does not itself tell us anything about what causes them, or justify categorising them as brain disorders.

## THE ROLE OF SEROTONIN

A neurotransmitter called serotonin is involved in a range of processes in our bodies, including in the brain.[153,154] Serotonin carries messages between nerve cells, and usually, once it has done its job, it is reabsorbed by the nerve cells (called 'reuptake'). Over the years, there has been a great deal of media interest in drugs known as selective serotonin reuptake inhibitors (SSRIs), including fluoxetine (often known by the brand name Prozac) and paroxetine (often known by the brand name Seroxat). These drugs increase the availability of serotonin in the brain by blocking natural biological mechanisms which would otherwise cause reuptake.

However, despite extensive research, there is no evidence that an abnormality in serotonin causes depression or that certain people are genetically predisposed to produce too little serotonin and therefore to experience depression.[155] It is possible that any change in serotonin is a physical sign that someone has been under stress. We do know that long-term exposure to cortisol, the stress hormone, is associated with reduced serotonin levels.[156,157]

> For me, depression goes hand in hand with anxiety.
>
> **Member of Survivors of Depression in Transition (SODIT) group**

Understanding depression

## STRESS, DRUGS AND ALCOHOL

One research study[158] found that 40 per cent of people with a diagnosis of long-lasting 'major depressive disorder' had a history of alcohol problems, and 60 per cent of people with long-lasting alcohol problems also had a history of long-lasting depression. This could be partly because we sometimes try to cope with depression by drinking, or because heavy drinking causes a lowering of mood, or a combination of the two.[159]

### ADDICTIONS

Drugs, alcohol and gambling can affect the way we experience reward, pleasure and inhibition or self-control. This can then foster further drug use or gambling in the quest for a 'high' but can lead to low mood when we lose at gambling or cannot get the drug. One researcher describes this as 'the dark side of addiction'.[160] It can become a vicious circle, whereby drinking, drug-taking or gambling becomes increasingly compulsive. People also sometimes get into a negative spiral of further depression and despair and use these kinds of behaviours to try to numb the pain.[161]

### DIET

People's circumstances can make it difficult to have a healthy diet. Yet, if we don't get the right nutrients, vitamins and minerals in our daily diet (for example omega-3 oils, folic acid, vitamin B12, chromium and magnesium) we can start to experience fatigue which in combination with other stresses can lead to depression.[162,163,164,165,166,167] Replacing these minerals can be helpful. However, it is important to consult a doctor, since taking large doses of vitamins and minerals bought over the counter can be expensive, and in some cases, harmful.

## SEASONAL DEPRESSION

Some people feel low in winter, and it has been suggested that this might be partly due to lack of sunlight.[168] The theory is that lower levels of light increase the secretion of a hormone called melatonin, which causes us to feel lethargic. Medical professionals sometimes use the term 'seasonal affective disorder' (SAD) to describe this. As with other things that contribute to depression, light levels probably play a role for some people, but are rarely the whole story. Seasonal depression may not happen only in winter – the return of any season during which a major loss or trauma happened can also bring seasonal depression.

### EXERCISE

In industrialised societies, many of us are not getting nearly enough exercise. Most of us don't make a conscious choice not to exercise; it's often just not necessary for daily life in the way it was for previous generations. A recent review of studies covering nearly 200,000 people across many different countries found that people are more likely to become depressed if they spend a lot of time sitting down watching television or using computers.[169] Several of these studies also seem to rule out the possibility that it was depression causing people to spend more time doing these things, rather than the other way around. Of course, these findings are generalisations and watching soothing daytime television can be a helpful distraction to give some respite from painful thoughts and feelings but it can reach a point at which it becomes part of the problem.

# A 'DEPRESSOGENIC' SOCIETY

A key message of this report is that depression is a very difficult but common human experience, but also an understandable one. In particular, it highlights how the events and circumstances of our lives often play a powerful role; countering the misleading but widespread idea that depression is usually the result of something going wrong in the brain. There are many aspects of our current society that can play a role. Some of these influences have been around for a long time – abuse, bullying, humiliation, loss, exploitation, marginalisation and experiences that make us feel we have failed. Others are relatively new and may be linked to new ideas or technologies which underestimate the importance of human connections, personal meaning, values, hope and creativity.[170] Changes in our social norms and values promote an expectation that individuals are solely responsible for their own success or lack of it which can lead to a sense of inadequacy in a social context.[171] Perhaps the most important social issue impacting on our mental health is pervasive inequality. Unequal societies are bad for our physical health, bad for social cohesion and very bad for our mental health.[172,173]

Understanding depression

# Part 3: Our mental health services and depression

# Part 3: Our mental health services and depression

> Actually depression can be a state of such pain you become numb to all life and then even your own has no worth. The breakthrough comes with maybe one person or contact or sometimes with many things that you have connected with. The important thing is connection.
>
> **Steph**

## KEY POINTS

We are currently over-reliant on medication to deal with depression. Medication can be helpful for some people. However, it can have unwanted as well as positive effects, and many people find it hard to come off.

Services should be structured and managed to ensure that mental health workers have time and space to listen.

Our services should be co-produced and culturally sensitive: managed and delivered by people who have experience of being 'on the receiving end' as well as mental health professionals.

Electro-convulsive therapy (ECT) has psychological effects which can be significant and unhelpful.

Therapy should be based on an individual understanding of our difficulties, collaboratively arrived at by the person and the psychologist or other mental health professional working together.

> Medication can help bring you to a level where you are able to engage with other therapies or activities.
>
> **Member of Survivors of Depression in Transition (SODIT) group**

Some people, particularly if they experience severe or long-lasting depression, find antidepressant medication helpful, either on its own or used alongside other approaches.[174]

Others take a different view. Professionals working in health care hold a wide range of views about medication; many feel that it is widely overprescribed and unhelpful on balance for many people. Psychiatrist Joanna Moncrieff has suggested that the term 'antidepressant' is misleading,[175] pointing out from her detailed examination of research literature that there is no evidence that the medication corrects any biological abnormality. She has argued that taking these prescribed drugs actually creates, rather than corrects, an abnormal brain state.[176] This, she argues, may help people to cope with some of their difficulties, in the same way that alcohol or sedatives may temporarily lessen social anxiety, but it does not solve the underlying problem.[177] Moncrieff accepts that medication can sometimes be helpful for people who are in distress, but points out that it does not 'cure' depression in the way that some physical illnesses can be cured – and that it doesn't help us to understand or address the reasons that a person became depressed in the first place, or what is keeping the depression going.[178,179]

Various organisations, including the British Medical Association (BMA), The Royal College of General Practitioners (RCGP) and Public Health England (PHE) have expressed concern about dependence-forming medications, including antidepressants.[180]

The UK government has asked PHE to carry out a public-health focused review of these commonly prescribed medicines for adults.[181] National Institute for Health and Clinical Excellence (NICE) guidelines for depression in adults[182] do not recommend medication for the majority of those experiencing depression. Instead, they recommend a range of alternative approaches – exercise and improving sleep, taking time off from work, self-help materials and psychological therapies. Antidepressant medication is recommended alongside psychological therapies for 'moderate to severe depression' in adults. For children and young people, NICE guidelines[183] state that medication should not be used for initial treatment with mild depression and evidence-based psychological intervention should be the first approach. A combined approach of psychological therapy and medication may be considered for moderate to severe depression after multidisciplinary review.

## PROBLEMS WITH MEDICATION

Many drugs have unwanted effects (also called adverse effects or side effects) as well as desired ones. Selective serotonin reuptake inhibitors (SSRIs) are often the first choice of medication that may be prescribed when people are depressed because they are thought to have fewer side effects than most other types of medication that could be prescribed. However, adverse effects are reported and one of the most frequent for SSRIs is sexual dysfunction.[184,185] Useful information and discussion about adverse effects, the effectiveness of medications and the way

Understanding depression

they work, is available from the website of the Council for Evidence Based Psychiatry (www.cepuk.org).

Worryingly, research has found that a significant number of people have difficulty stopping the drugs because of withdrawal effects, which can be severe and long-lasting.[186] Being prescribed medication may also reinforce the idea that people are 'ill', and that it is medication that makes things better. This can give the misleading message that there is little that people can do to help themselves and each other.

## COLLABORATIVE DECISIONS ABOUT MEDICATION

Some medical health professionals suggest that SSRIs should be used very sparingly, only for acute and severe depression,[187] and with a firm plan for tapering them off again after a short time.[188] No prescriber is in a position to know whether medication will help a particular individual, and if so which one, at which dose, or taken at which times. People need honest information and to be able to talk through options and try different things to see what helps.

Depressed people need to weigh up the costs and benefits of medication, as we do for all medication. Informed consent regarding all the various issues (including potential physical, emotional and psychological effects) is vital. A possible danger is that where medication seems to be the only concrete thing they can offer people, professionals may emphasise the benefits without fully discussing the potential negatives. For consent to be fully informed, both benefits and drawbacks need to be considered. You can get further information to help you weigh the benefits of any medication against its potential dangers and to inform your discussions and choice from RxISK[189], a free, independent medication safety website.

Important note: It can be dangerous to stop medication suddenly if you have been taking it for some time. Always discuss your decision with a doctor. See www.mind.org.uk for advice.[190]

Yes, I still use medication and have done for over 30 years, some has made me worse, it's true, but with the RIGHT support and education it can be a life saver.

**Steph**

# A PSYCHOLOGICAL VIEW ON ELECTRO-CONVULSIVE THERAPY (ECT)

Electro-convulsive therapy is sometimes used for people whose depression is severe or long-lasting. It involves sending electrical currents through the brain to bring on an epileptic fit. There is no agreed theory as to how this might reduce depression, and for reasons outlined below, many psychologists express concern about its use.[191,192]

ECT is carried out under general anaesthetic. A muscle relaxant is also given because, before this safeguard was introduced, muscle clenching during the fit sometimes caused injury. Despite what many people assume, ECT is still frequently used in mental health services. It is difficult to establish reliable figures on the current use of ECT as its use is no longer routinely audited. The last NHS survey in the UK in the early 2000s indicated about 11,000 people a year were given ECT in the UK, many of them aged over 65.[193] ECT is not recommended for children under 11 with depression and should be used extremely rarely for young people[194]. Freedom of information requests sent to NHS Trusts in England between 2011 and 2015 indicated that the number of people receiving ECT in England annually is between 2100 and 2700 and falling, though these figures are not for the whole UK and are likely to be an underestimate. The report[195] used the figures provided by services and found large variations in usage rates between Trusts. Most recipients were likely to be women (66 per cent) and over 60 years of age (56 per cent). More than a third (39 per cent) was given without consent. The report's authors concluded that an investigation into why ECT is still administered excessively to older people and women seems long overdue.

NICE guidelines[196] recommend ECT only in cases where an adult is very severely depressed and thought to be at grave risk of imminent death through suicide or self-neglect, and where psychological therapy has already been tried as well as several different drugs. NICE does not recommend ECT for children in any circumstances.[197]

From a psychological perspective, although some people report that ECT is helpful in alleviating depression, it is likely that this is because of the physical after-effects of the induced fit and/or powerful placebo effects[199,200], rather than resolving any underlying issues relevant to depression. Further, up to a third of people who undergo ECT report that it was a very distressing experience.[201,202,]We agree with the relevant NICE guidelines, [203] that ECT should never be used without informed consent and not used with children. Advance directives, which are written plans created at a time when a person is considered to have capacity to make decisions, can be used to specify a person's wishes about ECT and referred to at a later time when the person is considered to lack capacity. Any later lack of capacity to consent should not be used to override their stated wishes.

> It's not a traumatic experience. That's an absolute myth. You're out for the count then you wake up feeling quite safe. [...] But I have paid a heavy price. I've lost almost all of my long-term memory, and memory is the most precious thing we have. [...] I have no recollection of my children growing up or my first wife. My memories have all been created by looking at photographs.[198]

> A collective partnership is the way forward and the 'power dynamics' must be equalised.
>
> **Member of Survivors of Depression in Transition (SODIT) group**

'Co-production' is about developing more equal partnerships between people who use services, their informal carers and professionals.[204] This can be challenging for existing service providers as new ideas can be very different to what has traditionally been provided. Some of the most innovative and popular services are those which are designed and led by people with personal experience of being on the receiving end. Typically, these projects are characterised by being collaborative, respectful and welcoming of difference.

**Below are some examples of user-led services:**

*The Nottingham Mind Medication and Wellbeing Group*[205] helps people who want to explore ways to reduce their use of psychiatric medication.[206]

*SODIT* – which stands for Survivors of Depression in Transition – is a peer support group based in Sheffield.

*Leeds Survivor Led Crisis Service (LSLCS)*[207,208] provides a place of sanctuary and support, as an alternative to hospital admission and other statutory services, for people in acute mental health crisis. It is governed and managed by people with direct experience of mental health problems.[209]

The *Safe Haven Café* in Aldershot[210] provides mental health support in a relaxed environment and acts as a hub for people to support each other. It provides an effective alternative to mainstream mental health services.

The *Mind YASP* (Young Adults Service and Projects) *Café* in Manchester[211] is an internet café for young people aged 15–25. It provides mental health support such as counselling, mentoring and befriending. Many of its volunteer staff have also experienced mental health problems and may themselves have used the support offered at the café.[212]

User-led initiatives often represent the best, most flexible, responsive and appropriate ways of meeting needs of particular groups.

> 'Being with people who themselves have experienced depression in a peer support setting, is, well I can say amazing! This has given me genuine human connections with women who do not have to say a thing... they just know.'
>
> **Member of Survivors of Depression in Transition (SODIT) group**

## MAKING TIME AND SPACE TO LISTEN

Increasingly, NHS staff, including clinical psychologists, counselling psychologists and psychological therapists are feeling pressurised themselves.[213] None the less, despite the pressures on our NHS services, when we engage with mental health services, we should expect to receive kindness and compassion and be provided empathic, listening care. An accompanying paper with suggestions is in preparation and the excellent book *Intelligent Kindness*[214] considers these issues in detail.

> When formulation has been co-created it has been very helpful and, if used as an organic document or diagram, helps understand the issues and more importantly, the solutions to work on.
>
> **Member of Survivors of Depression in Transition (SODIT) group**

## FORMULATION: TELLING YOUR STORY AND MAKING SENSE OF YOUR EXPERIENCES

When people are depressed, it is vital that they are able to tell the story of their experiences and make sense of them and are supported to make any changes they decide on. These stories and understandings, developed collaboratively between the person and a professional helper, are sometimes referred to as 'formulations' and should guide all help and treatment. Professionals need to consider people's cultural background in order to understand and respond helpfully to their distress. This is an area where psychologists can make a big contribution because collaborative formulation is a central element of the training of clinical and counselling psychologists.

We describe formulation in more detail in Part 4 of this document and suggest ways to promote and support it in our accompanying publication for service commissioners (in preparation).

Understanding depression

# Part 4: What can help if you are depressed –
# Getting to a better place

PART 4

# Part 4: What can help if you are depressed – Getting to a better place

**KEY POINTS**

Depression is an experience of human distress. Thinking of it as an illness is only one way of thinking about it, with advantages and disadvantages.

Looking after your physical health is an important first step: exercising, eating well and cultivating good sleep habits.

Our friends, family, colleagues and communities are often the most important sources of support and help.

If there are practical problems to be solved, for example at work or school, or if people have experienced abuse or financial difficulties, these should usually be addressed first. It is important for professionals to help with practical as well as emotional issues.

Issues of meaning are often central to depression. For some, this is expressed through their questions around spirituality.

Psychological therapies are helpful for many people and so it is a good idea to try them if they are made available.

A psychological formulation based on the experiences, goals and aspirations of the individual experiencing depression is central to recovery and helps to guide actions towards getting to a better place.

> Depression for me manifested as a deep sense of loss: a loss of meaning and purpose. I didn't feel that I was where I wanted to be, but also I had no clear idea of what a better place or situation would look like. 'Recovery', then, meant 'recovery of life' – a restoration of my sense of significance as an individual and the feeling of meaningful connection to the world around me.
>
> **Emily**

## RECOGNITION OF DISTRESS

Before people can do anything to help themselves, they or sometimes someone close to them, need to recognise their predicament. Sometimes people do not realise they are in distress or depressed and, for many reasons, just get on with life because they have to. It may take them or others time and experience before they or someone else realise that help is needed.

> At some stages of my life it has been helpful to think of depression as an illness. It is when I am ill that services are most likely to offer me help and support. This is usually medication. Which helps at times of great stress. However, there have been other times when I would rather think of depression as something we all experience from time to time. This helps me take the heat out of the label and work with it in a more creative way.
>
> **Laura**

## A RESPONSE TO DISTRESS, NOT A DISEASE

The most important message of this report is that depression is not a disease but a human experience: a complex, understandable set of psychological responses to the events and circumstances of our lives. It is understandable in both evolutionary and psychological terms and has a function: it often tells us that things need to change in some way. When we are depressed, we don't necessarily need 'treatment'. However, we may well need practical support, and perhaps help to make changes – both small, short-term ones to help get 'unstuck', and sometimes larger ones too. In addition, an important message of this document is that it may be unhelpful to always assume that 'the problem' lies within the person who is struggling with low mood. Some forms of oppression are very common in parts of our society and not easy to address but it can be a helpful first step to notice and name this when we are able to.

There are many things that can help, and no single approach will offer a complete or universal solution to the various problems that can lead to depression. Some people may have underlying physical problems (such as anaemia, thyroid problems or nutritional deficiencies) that need to be addressed.

In the absence of the above physical problems, and where it is difficult to pin down causes, some people find 'antidepressant' medication helpful, although, as mentioned in the medication section above, not everyone thinks it is helpful and many believe it is overprescribed.[215] Physical exercise may be helpful if a person's daily routine involves a lot of sitting and not much moving, since our bodies evolved to move more than most of us do today. Many people find psychological therapies helpful. However, in many cases, the main thing that helps is what psychologist David Smail called 'comfort, clarification and encouragement':[216,217] others who care and who listen, who help us to work out what is contributing to our distress and where changes might be possible: people who help and support us to make those changes, or who can offer necessary practical support. This can come from counselling or therapy, but it can also come from each other. As we have mentioned in earlier sections of this report, our communities (geographic and others) have

a huge role to play, not only through people supporting each other emotionally but in joining together in social action to make or campaign for changes that are not just down to us individually to make.

This section describes a number of things that different people find helpful. They are possible starting points for thinking about what might be helpful when people are depressed. As the Scottish Recovery Network[218] puts it: 'Recovery is being able to live a meaningful and satisfying life, as defined by each person… Each individual's recovery, like his or her experience of the mental health problems or illness, is a unique and deeply personal process.' We start with some individual things because they are important, but then we broaden it out again to the societies and communities that are crucial to human flourishing.

> Recovery is a journey not a destination.
>
> **Member of Survivors of Depression in Transition (SODIT) group**

## PHYSICAL FACTORS

### DIET

Some studies have suggested that where someone's diet has been poor, restoring levels of vitamins and minerals can be helpful.[219,220,221] A blood test can establish whether someone is iron or zinc deficient, for example, so that they can add these to their diet or take supplements if appropriate.

### SLEEP

There is a close relationship between sleep and mental health. Sleep repairs and restores our bodies and brains and is vital for wellbeing. Establishing a regular sleep routine is important, as is the place we sleep, which needs to be comfortable and relaxing. MIND gives advice on sleep[222] and the Mental Health

Foundation has published a report on the impact of sleep on health and wellbeing.[223]

### EXERCISE

National Institute for Health and Clinical Excellence (NICE) guidelines recommend structured programmes of physical activity to help with depression.[224] A recent review found that programmes of exercise tailored to individual people's situations can be as helpful as medication for many people experiencing both mild and severe depression.[225] Exercise can also be helpful in reducing depression after giving birth.[226]

This does not need to be intensive – gentle exercise such as walking can be just as beneficial for wellbeing as more strenuous exercise. The important thing is to do some form of physical activity on a regular basis.

## MINDFULNESS

There is an increasing evidence base which supports mindfulness as a practice which can help to bring about a calm state of body and mind and prevent depression. Mindfulness can be defined as 'a way to pay attention on purpose, in the present moment, and nonjudgmentally.'[227] Mindfulness is recommended by NICE to prevent recurrences of depression. Mindfulness can form part of Mindfulness based Cognitive Therapy which is a psychological therapy (see section below).

## YOGA

According to a review, several research studies[228] have suggested that yoga can be helpful for people experiencing depression. While some people see yoga mainly as a form of exercise, for many it is also a spiritual practice and an opportunity to develop greater awareness of our bodies and minds.

# THE POWER OF RELATIONSHIPS AND COMMUNITY

The community – our own existing network of relationships, and new ones that we develop – is the most important source of help for many people, although it is often overlooked in favour of a focus on therapies or medication and on the individual. Whatever the nature of someone's difficulties, the most important things are those we all need – supportive relationships, good housing, freedom from constant money or other worries, enjoyable and meaningful things to do, and a valued role within our communities.

The Mental Health Foundation's *Strategies for Living* project asked people with mental health problems what helps them most.[229] Significantly, it was generally not treatment that people found most helpful, but everyday things. Relationships with professionals and therapists were helpful, but more important were relationships with friends, family and other significant people such as work colleagues – people with whom we spend much more time. The support of other people who have experienced mental health problems was often also very important. Medication was helpful for some people but for others, other things were more important, for example religious or spiritual beliefs, or making changes in their lives.

Moreover, studies have shown that depression can be reduced through a focus on social identity, since a sense of belonging to groups helps us to interpret our actions in less negative terms.[230] Similarly, a review of studies of what people find helpful for recovery identified five main themes: connectedness, hope, identity, meaning and empowerment.[231] Key aspects of these themes included receiving support from others with similar experiences and building relationships or being involved in a community. Importantly, people said they did not want to be 'propped up' by others; most people wanted to contribute as well. What can often help most is an opportunity to contribute in whatever way feels possible at the time.[232]

Of course, not all relationships and communities are supportive. If we find ourselves in a negative situation that is unlikely to change, it might be best to disengage and move on, if we can. Talking things over with a friend or counsellor is often a helpful first step.

## HOW FRIENDS AND FAMILY CAN HELP

The way our society is organised means that loneliness is a big problem for many people, and particularly people from marginalised groups as we discuss in Part 2 and below. But even those people who have friends and family around often feel alone, helpless and pessimistic when they are depressed. People may find themselves drifting away from family or friends and some people find they can make things feel worse. So, for many people, one of the most powerful first steps to take is to talk to someone about what they're going through: a friend, family member or colleague, or perhaps a GP, counsellor or faith leader. It means they're no longer alone and can begin to unpick what might be causing depression and keeping it going.

The main thing is to find someone who will really listen to how things are and not just rush to try and reassure that things will be OK. When someone is in the grip of deep depression, someone else saying that everything will be fine can sound hollow and unfeeling – as if they don't understand what the person is going through. While it's good to talk to people who know that we can get through our difficulties, it helps if they don't feel an urgency to impose that belief on us.

To be there for someone else, we need to be in a reasonably good state ourselves, so the person confided in may themselves need support. Often the stressful events that have led to a person becoming depressed are ones that also affect a whole family or community, so everyone is dealing with increased stress. Psychological support which takes account of all the family members affected by depression could be very helpful in these circumstances.[233]

When we are stressed it can be more difficult to feel caring towards someone else.[234] MIND provides guidance for family members who are uncertain how to support someone.[235] The *Carers Trust* has also developed a concept called the *Triangle of Care*.[236] This is a collaborative approach that recognises the importance of professionals working together with friends and family to help someone who is experiencing depression. However, stigma can be a barrier to help seeking for both someone experiencing depression and their families. Also, the way depression is experienced and understood within a family system will influence how support is provided. A review[237] which highlighted these issues suggested different types of support will be helpful at different stages for couples and/or families affected by depression.

Occasionally, family members may discourage people from seeking help outside the immediate family, either because they have ideas about what's wrong that they feel outsiders won't share or understand,[238] or because they fear that revealing difficulties will bring shame on the family. Friends, family members, work colleagues, members of your mosque, church, temple or other place of worship or even professionals often have a whole range of views, and it makes sense to choose carefully who to talk to when feeling low.

> ...Accessing help can be difficult and the response of the services can make matters worse... If you love someone who has a mental health issue, most likely you desperately ... want to see peace, pleasure, wellbeing and resilience flourish in that person. It's true that some of us are more skilled than others at knowing how to help. It's human to make mistakes but [for the carer] the mental illness and the mental health service magnify the mistakes... so often the information isn't there... it's not provided... It leads to family breakdown.
>
> **Anon, in position of carer[239]**

> There is a definite stigma towards mental health problems in my community... Nobody seemed to want to understand about my diaganosis [of depression] and I didn't feel I could talk to anybody because people are not equipped to provide support. They believe in leaving it to the power of prayer.
>
> **Anon from contributions used in development of NICE guidelines[240]**

## THE WIDER COMMUNITY: CLUBS, HOBBIES, SOCIETIES AND COMMUNITY ARTS

There is no one single route to better mental health. Each of us is different and different things help different people. People who have had some support from psychological or counselling services or perhaps a mental health service team, may be able to use a 'formulation' (see the section on this later in Part 4) to help decide what to concentrate on first. For some people, local faith groups are helpful, as can organised local volunteering. Exercise or sport can be important, especially if done with others, perhaps as part of a local club or association. Community arts projects can be good for self-expression as well as a way of connecting with others. [241,242,243,244] With many such projects run by not-for-profit arts organisations, the focus may not be explicitly on mental health but they can still be hugely helpful when experiencing mental health difficulties. Singing in a local choir or 'singing for health' groups have also been shown to lift mood and to have significant health benefits.[245]

To link with others who experience depression, there are local and national self-help groups such as MIND. There are links to these and other organisations in the 'Useful resources, reading and organisations' section of this document.

> What pain is within you, you can sing it out – women's choir for me is an outlet, it's great for your mental wellbeing.
>
> **June**

## SELF-SOOTHING

Self-soothing is all about comforting, nurturing and being kind to ourselves.[246] Whilst some may recognise that they already use strategies that work in this way to help cope with overwhelming and distressing feelings, others may never have learnt how to self soothe. Most self-help approaches suggest simple steps that can often really help in difficult situations. If possible, it can be helpful to stop what we are doing, step back and observe what is really happening. It may then be possible to think about what can be controlled in the situation and what is beyond control. Reminding ourselves of what is really important, and our values can be helpful emotionally in the midst of chaos. We also need to be kind to ourselves and our bodies. It may be helpful to think of soothing each of our five senses: vision, hearing, smell, taste and touch. Often simple things can make us feel better, for example, going for a walk and taking time to see things we appreciate such as plants, flowers or clouds, listening to music we like, or feeling the soft water on our skin from a bath or shower. It's worth trying out different things linked to various senses to see what feels comfortable and seems to work best. It can also take time and practice to believe that we can usually rely on something soothing to help us to feel better. Some online links offer suggestions for ways to self soothe in the resources section.

## GROWING FROM EXPERIENCE

Issues of meaning and growth are often central to depression. Instead of thinking about depression as a problem, the experience could be seen as a healthy 'call to change' and something which can lead to growth and development. Emotional suffering can be seen as an important part of life which gives us information that we need to know to help us develop. It may also alert us to the fact that something significant in our environment needs to change. If we understand and manage it thoughtfully, we can make use of it and our suffering becomes 'productive' by helping us and potentially others to grow and change for the better.[247,248,249,250]

## SPIRITUAL DEVELOPMENT

So whatever turmoil or turbulence life presents to you, know that it happened for a reason; you broke down so that you may wake up. You got lost so that you may find yourself again.[251]

Some people come to see their experiences of depression as a spiritual crisis and an essential part of discovering what is really important to them in their lives.[252] For many people, exploration of these issues and their spiritual growth and development is a valued part of their recovery. Again, being part of a supportive community can be useful and provide invaluable practical and emotional support.[253] This doesn't necessarily have to involve organised religion. Different people find a sense of spiritual meaning or connection in different ways, for example through nature, art, music or poetry. It can be helpful to link with others who have similar beliefs to ourselves to support us to find personal meaning and connections.

However, as with any group, a religious community or elements of it might have been part of the problem. If this is the case, it can be helpful to connect in a different way or with a different community.

'For me, my faith and sense of community and support that is church, I am loved and cared for – helps me stay strong... I believe in God, helped me dealing with loneliness. It's a comfort to have someone/something bigger and stronger than me with me.'

CK

As outlined in this report, people become depressed for different reasons. If practical problems are involved – money worries, say, or problems at work or school, it often makes sense to focus on them first. It may seem obvious that addressing these practical things is important, but they can be overlooked, particularly if depression is viewed solely as an individual problem. Here we list some common areas where such support may be needed.

## WORK

Work is important for many reasons. Apart from the obvious financial one, work is often an important source of social support and also contributes to our sense of identity.

### Reasonable adjustments

Many people conceal depression or other mental health problems from employers or education institutions, for fear of discrimination. However, in many countries, people who declare a mental health difficulty have particular rights under employment law.[254]

In the UK, employees can ask for 'reasonable adjustments'. Examples might include a phased return to work after a period of leave, or working 10am to 6pm instead of 9am to 5pm if taking medication that makes it hard to get going in the morning.

### Support for improving a bad work situation

If work is part of the reason you have become depressed, then these issues need to be addressed. You can get advice from a trade union or Citizens' Advice, and employers should have policies on dignity at work, disability and equality rights.[255,256,257,258]

Sometimes returning to work takes careful planning. A letter from the GP can help, as can human resources departments in large organisations. If a person decides that the job probably wasn't suitable in the first place, there are a number of possible sources of help with finding somewhere where they will thrive:

a friend, counsellor, therapist, life coach or careers advisor.

### Help to find and keep a suitable job

If someone has mental health difficulties and wants to work but is currently unemployed, Individual Placement and Support (IPS) services,[259] where available, can help them find and keep a suitable job. The IPS worker will ask what they are looking for in a job, and help with applications for jobs that the person can see themself doing and would like to do. Where appropriate, they can also offer support to the employer, and help to put in place any arrangements that are needed to help the new employee to give their best and stay in the job.

There are currently IPS projects in London, Sussex and the West Midlands. Plans are underway to extend this to six more regions including Berkshire, Lincolnshire and Bradford. However, a recent evaluation undertaken in Essex suggested the IPS scheme there was less helpful than hoped in terms of supporting people with mental health difficulties moving into and out of work.[260] The report suggested that some service users felt pressure from Job Centre Plus to get a job. IPS as originally conceived was not about putting any pressure on people. It is about supporting people to realise their aspirations. A recent study demonstrated that when vocational NHS service developments are grounded in what service users say helps them (person-centred, networked and co-ordinated approaches) people can achieve their vocational goals.[261]

Although meaningful work is good for wellbeing, some people have such significant mental health problems that they are not able to undertake a paid job. Others are able to at some times and not others. Bad jobs are also often worse for mental health than unemployment.[262,263] We view it as a matter of significant concern that some current government policies (at least in England) appear to be based on a view that most people should be able to work and that those who do not feel able to are likely to be exaggerating their difficulties.

There is evidence that for some people claiming benefits, the pressure and repeated assessments they experience from agencies employed by the Department for Work and Pensions are very detrimental to their mental health.[264] Most people want to work, but it makes no sense either for the employee or the employer for people to take unsuitable jobs. We need to find ways to support people to manage work that uses their skills in ways that are best for them.

### RETIREMENT FROM WORK

For many of us our work is an important part of our identity[265], so retiring from work can present challenges. Getting older and retirement both involve changes in lifestyle and it's important to take care of mental and physical health.[266] We are likely to need time to appreciate the significance of the change. It can be helpful to think of other ways we can continue to develop our self-identity and connection to our communities, for instance volunteering, learning a new skill or trying something we've always wanted to do but never had the time.

### EDUCATION AND TRAINING

School, college and university can be good for our mental health: all provide a sense of structure, contact with other students, and purpose and direction. However, they can also be stressful and it can be difficult to concentrate or progress if you are feeling low. Flexible individual arrangements and support are often needed and can make all the difference.

#### School and college

It may not always be immediately obvious when children and young people are feeling depressed. They may become withdrawn, avoidant and tearful, or angry and defiant. The most important thing is that the young person feels understood and supported and knows that there is someone they can turn to if they are worried, stressed or unwell. If they have been off school or college, they might need help to catch up with learning.

There are links to some helpful organisations in the 'Useful resources, reading and organisations' section of this document although this age group is not the primary focus of this publication and alternative resources with a focus on the health of children and young people should be considered.

#### University

There is a wide variety of student services to help people experiencing depression. 'Students Against Depression'[267] is a web-based resource with ideas and links. Most academic departments have a personal tutor system or another method for arranging pastoral care for students. Tutors can help guide students to counselling services or mental health advisors, and also help them to plan workload and breaks when needed. Formal peer support schemes are available at some universities, consisting of student volunteers trained to provide listening and support and to refer on if necessary.

Nightline is a student listening service based on the Samaritans model, providing a source of anonymous and confidential support through the night. Look on your campus intranet or noticeboards for contact details.

#### Life long learning

Our education doesn't stop when we become adults. The purpose of adult education can be vocational, social, recreational or for self-development[268] and for all these reasons it can help to prevent depression.

### FINANCIAL DIFFICULTIES

Many people have financial difficulties which can be ongoing. Money difficulties and mental health are often linked and there are resources which can advise and help.[269] For example, if benefits are sanctioned or a person loses their home they are likely to become depressed and anxious. If you are struggling with debt, there are organisations that offer free support and advice and can help you work out the best thing to do. In the UK these include Citizen's Advice[270] and National Debtline.[271]

## HOW THE CURRENT SYSTEM WORKS: 'DIAGNOSTIC' CATEGORIES

When someone first tells a GP that they are feeling depressed, they will probably be asked how low their mood is, what other problems they are experiencing, and how long they have felt this way.[272,273,274,275] GPs and other medical professionals tend to think in terms of diagnostic categories, so they might be assessing whether the person fits the criteria for, say 'clinical depression' or 'major depressive disorder'. These labels don't tell us about the nature or causes of our problems; they really only mean that the professional thinks the problems are significant enough to warrant some kind of help. They are about classifying rather than explaining, and the cut-offs are relatively arbitrary. 'Clinical depression' is not a different kind from 'ordinary depression'. It just means a person's mood is considered lower than a certain point. However, our current mental health services are based on these categories. So, if someone has felt depressed every day for two weeks and finds it difficult to get on with their normal daily activities, they may be given a diagnosis of 'clinical depression' or 'depressive disorder' and offered medication or other professional help. The *Improving Access to Psychological Therapies* (IAPT) programme for adults in England has helped more people access services, but many people still find it difficult to get help.

Health professionals in England and Wales are encouraged by NICE[276] to use one of two standard diagnostic (i.e. categorisation) frameworks: either the International Classification of Diseases (ICD-10) or the Diagnostic and Statistical Manual of the American Psychiatric Association (DSM-5). These are essentially guidelines for categorising people's problems according to their type (e.g. low mood or anxiety) and severity. If someone's problems reach a predetermined threshold of severity and/or duration, they may be offered treatment (usually psychological therapy or medication, or a combination of both).

For example, using the ICD-10 system, a diagnosis of 'depressive disorder' is made if three criteria are met:

> Firstly, the person is experiencing persistent sadness or low mood, or loss of interests or pleasure, or fatigue or low energy, and

> Secondly, this has been the case most days, for most of the time, for at least two weeks, and

> Thirdly, they are also experiencing at least four of the following: disturbed sleep, poor concentration or indecisiveness, low self-confidence, poor or increased appetite, suicidal thoughts or acts, agitation or slowing of movements, or guilt or self-blame.

Drawing on a list of 10 possible 'symptoms' (thoughts, feelings and behaviours), the GP or other medical professional will classify the level of depression as either 'absent' (fewer than four symptoms), 'mild' (four symptoms), 'moderate' (five to six) or 'severe' (seven or more symptoms). The DSM-5 list is similar, but its list also includes gaining or losing weight in a short time.

Psychiatric diagnosis is a contested practice in mental health services. Critics suggest that labels like 'depressive disorder' are misleading in that they imply that an underlying illness has been identified, with a known cause, whereas this is not the case. They also argue that the labels can unhelpfully medicalise problems that arise from the events and circumstances of our lives. They point out that labels can be used to remove human rights, for example detaining people in hospital and giving them medication against their will. Despite the problems, within our current system people often find that they need a diagnosis in order to get help and support, and to access welfare benefits. Whenever a diagnosis is used, for the process to be helpful, it needs to be collaborative.[277] Everyone should also have the right to describe and make sense of their problems in the way that is most helpful for

them. No one has all the answers, particularly in this controversial area.

The Division of Clinical Psychology of the British Psychological Society has published a leaflet which explores the complexities and controversies of mental health 'diagnosis' in more detail.[278]

## PSYCHOLOGICAL (TALKING) THERAPIES

Psychological help available on the NHS usually takes one of three forms: 'low intensity intervention', psychotherapy of one or other type, and help from a clinical or counselling psychologist.

### PSYCHOLOGICAL WELLBEING OR 'LOW-INTENSITY' INTERVENTIONS

For many people, relatively straightforward ('low intensity') psychological support is sufficient.

Many different 'low intensity' interventions are available. These may include: individual guided self-help based on cognitive-behavioural principles and including problem-solving techniques and behavioural activation (helping people overcome vicious circles of depression and inactivity); computerised CBT (cognitive behaviour therapy); structured group physical activity programmes; group-based psycho-education (information and explanation about depression), and peer support (support from someone who has themselves experienced depression in the past).

### SPECIFIC ONE-TO-ONE THERAPIES

People may be offered a specific therapy or given a choice; a variety of therapy options are available, some of which are recommended by NICE[279]. These include cognitive behaviour therapy (CBT), interpersonal therapy (IPT), psychodynamic psychotherapy, and mindfulness-based cognitive therapy (MBCT). These therapies are offered because NICE was able to establish that there was a reasonable level of evidence for their effectiveness. Currently, the NICE guideline for depression is under review. Groups of people who

represent different organisations (e.g. service users, professionals) have asked NICE to look at the long-term effects of therapies rather than just the short-term effects and to make recommendations which take this into account. Some reviews from other countries have considered this and suggest other types of therapies that can also be helpful.[280,281] A recent study looked at many different service user experiences of psychological therapies for depression and found that common features, such as enabling sharing and talking about feelings to others was seen as helpful, rather than a particular type of therapy. The study also noted that sometimes therapy could be unhelpful for people and highlighted the need for service users to be more involved in discussions and decisions, including tailoring therapy to individual needs and taking social and cultural contexts into account.[282]

In general, all psychological therapy depends on a trusting, collaborative working relationship between therapist and client. In some cases this is probably the most important 'ingredient',[283] and it is vital that people are able to find a therapist with whom they feel comfortable. Different approaches also suit different people, depending on their preferences and on what appears to be keeping the problem going – the 'formulation' described below. The different types of therapy have more in common than they have differences. All are essentially an opportunity for a conversation between two or more people, talking through the problems and working out what may be contributing and what might help. A good working relationship between the people involved is vital.

With all psychological therapies it is important to remember that:

Engaging with therapy is a choice. Where people feel that it is not for them, or not the right time, this should be respected.

Therapy can only be offered to people, not imposed or forced on them.

Therapy is not and should not be about a therapist doing something to you to make you better.

When someone is very depressed it may be hard to ask the therapist for what they want or do anything more than try to feel less down, but once they start feeling a bit more hopeful they can think together with the therapist about longer-term goals.

Therapy can sometimes be less helpful than hoped, and occasionally therapists can do harm. It is wise to make enquiries about qualifications and check professional registers particularly if seeking help outside the NHS.

Even an excellent therapist will not be a good fit for every client.

Even the most 'evidence-based' therapies don't help everyone. People themselves are the best judges of whether a particular therapy or therapist is helping them.

## SEEING A CLINICAL PSYCHOLOGIST OR A COUNSELLING PSYCHOLOGIST

As a result of their wide training, clinical and counselling psychologists are able to offer more flexibility than therapists trained in only one particular approach. Using their knowledge of the different kinds of things that can lead people to become depressed and of what can help, a psychologist will work with you to work out an understanding or 'formulation' of your particular situation. The formulation will suggest possible ways forward.

Transformation narratives emphasise the agency of the self in the healing process as opposed to crediting professionals with curative powers. In this light, the task of mental health professionals becomes one of supporting people and helping them build skills and a sense of agency. Helping people learn to become self-directing as opposed to compliant, is a goal of the recovery process.

**Pat Deegan[284]**

## PSYCHOLOGICAL FORMULATION

Psychological formulation is 'a process of on-going collaborative sense-making'[285] between the person and the psychologist or therapist. Together, they explore different aspects of the difficulties that were faced by the person: how these developed, how problems are maintained, the personal meaning of the events, relationships and circumstances of a person's life, and of their current distress. Formulations are hypotheses or ideas and not facts[286] (though facts and events may be included). In developing a formulation, a professional brings their knowledge and experience to helping consider the following kinds of question:

1. What are the problems as you see them?

2. How might some of the difficulties you are experiencing relate to one another?

3. How might these difficulties have developed over time, and what is maintaining them as problems now?

4. What is the personal meaning of past events or your current circumstances, and how does this understanding affect you?

5. What are your strengths, skills and resources?

6. What could help?

Formulations can help to describe problems and help to understand more about the links between any on-going stressors, personal strengths and social resources (be they among friends or family or in the wider community).

When enough of the story has been explored, the person and the therapist together may write a summary or draw a diagram as a way of noting some key points to have in mind for guiding therapy. Metaphors, stories, pictures and/or diagrams can be helpful in developing a formulation and this can be changed or adapted later if needed. The way in which formulations are presented will impact upon the way the ideas are understood and used

to negotiate meanings, so this needs careful consideration and collaboration between therapist and service user.[287]

Usually, a formulation is created jointly by the person with their psychologist or other mental health professional and discussed in the course of their meetings. Sometimes, it can be written in the form of a letter. It can also be re-written if this is helpful.

**Formulation for Miriam** [Not a real person but based on real people]

**Childhood**

You were born and grew up on the outskirts of a large town with your mum, dad and younger brother who was born three years after you. The family didn't have much money but you mostly enjoyed school and especially liked music and football.

When you were 11 years old, you found out that your mum had cancer. It was a very hard time and she had lots of operations and treatments. Sadly, your mum died three years later. Your dad started dating other women quite soon afterwards and you would stay in looking after your brother. There was no money for a baby-sitter. Your dad remarried when you were 16, around the time you left school. Although you remain in contact with your dad, you feel he is now more focused on his new life with his wife and her younger children.

**Work, friends and leaving home**

You were able to get a job soon after leaving school and have worked mainly in retail jobs with several large shops in town. You met Mick when you were 18, moving in to a rented flat with him a year later. You, Mick and friends used to enjoy yourselves at music gigs and festivals and watch football, which you also still played a bit. At first you were making ends meet as you both worked, but it was difficult to save. You had some thoughts about manager training as you felt you could contribute more and perhaps get paid more, but your boss didn't seem interested in discussing it, and Mick didn't see the point of taking on the stress of it. He seems relatively unambitious but you like his 'happy-go-lucky' style.

**Becoming a mother**

You kept working until the birth of your daughter when you were 22. Rhianna is now 18 months old and you have gone back to work for a few hours a week but you've been finding it really hard and you feel very tired and depressed. You and Mick manage to make ends meet and pay the bills but you worry about money and you no longer have time, energy or money to do the things you used to enjoy.

**Remembering childhood losses**

We have spoken about how you had to grow up quickly when you were 11 after your mum's diagnosis. You helped her, your dad and brother, and did a lot of cooking and cleaning around the house whilst she was having lots of treatments. It felt very frightening for you but you coped by keeping busy and doing all you could to help. When your dad started dating other women so soon after your mum's death, you were happy for him but also sad because you would have liked him to have spent more time with you and had some time to think about your mum and all that had happened and to be sad together. Your Dad also worked long hours to pay the bills.

You met Mick soon after leaving school and have a good relationship with him. However, you started to feel very sad after the birth of Rhianna when you would have really liked to have had your mother around. You started to miss her even more and it feels hard to talk about this with anyone.

**Feeling low and finding usual coping strategies don't work so well**

You have survived some very difficult times and have coped by keeping busy doing things you think could help. You now feel sad and tired and you find little things people say and do seem to trigger very strong emotional reactions in you (mainly anger) that you later feel bad about.

### Hopes for the future

You realise that you may need to re-visit some of your unprocessed feelings from the past. You hope to do this in individual therapy and you are thinking about whether you may be able to join a group of people who have also suffered losses. At the moment, you do not feel you really belong in some of the mother and toddler groups but you would like to be able to take Rhianna to some activities with children of her own age. When you feel stronger and have the resources, you hope to be able to spend time doing things you used to enjoy – like going to live music gigs and watching and playing football. Looking further ahead, you are thinking about whether you could work in a more satisfying job, with better prospects, but it seems impossible to think about that at all at the moment.

Formulations can also be drawn in different ways – see, for an example, the diagram on the following page, also for Miriam but highlighting some different and additional issues. In particular, the diagram version started from Miriam talking about tension in the house in the evenings, and some of her low mood being around this.

**Formulation diagram for Miriam: How Miriam's problems are linked**

PART 4

**Events that happen**
Young daughter Rhianna starts crying
Partner Mick gets home from work and asks why Rhianna cries so much

**Thoughts: How I interpret events**
I can't cope
I wish I still had my mum
Mick finds me boring now
It's all my fault – if I could work more hours we'd be able to have a baby-sitter
and go out more
Mick will leave me

**Underlying beliefs**
I'm useless
I'm a bad mother
I'm dull and boring
I'm not good enough to have a happy family
I cannot enjoy myself

**Sources of Inequality**
Learning from early experiences of low
family income;
Restricted choices.
Impact of social inequalities on current life choices

**Life experiences & Vulnerability Factors**
Mum's illness and death
Dad leaving me to look after brother Sam.
Living with Mick, working less and having daughter
(good and bad things about this)
Increased responsibility/change of role.

Increases stress

**Responses: What I do when this happens**
Get irritable with Rhianna
Argue with Mick when he gets home from work
Don't acknowledge/use my strengths
(e.g., music, skills in organising, sport)

**Feelings: How I feel**
Sad
Anxious
Stressed
Angry

Understanding depression

> What's recovery like? For me it was slow. It means being more able to see what's happened that has led to me feeling low, and better at talking kindly to myself, and better at asking for support or finding the places where I thrive and the people I can work with. Have I grown into someone new? Well, I am a very different person today than before my first diagnosis of depression.
>
> **Annie**

This formulation-led approach is conceptually very different from the traditional 'diagnostic' approach outlined earlier, which assigns people to categories of 'disorder'. A recent report from the United Nations Special Rappoteur suggests that rather than focusing on fixing 'chemical imbalances' perhaps the focus should be on 'power imbalances and inequalities'. [288]

The British Psychological Society's Division of Clinical Psychology has outlined the first steps of an alternative to the medicalised approach to distress. This 'Power Threat Meaning Framework' uses four key questions as a basis for identifying patterns in the way psychological distress is experienced and expressed. The questions are:

1. 'What has happened to you?' (How has Power operated in your life?)

2. 'How did it affect you?' (What kind of Threats does this pose?)

3. 'What sense did you make of it?' (What is the Meaning of these situations and experiences to you?)

4. 'What did you have to do to survive?' (What kinds of Threat Response are you using?)

'Power' includes different things and can be about the many examples of abuse, trauma and discrimination, both within relationships and within wider society, which have been discussed in this document. In Miriam's case, as often is so, power operated in a subtle way, in that she felt that she should adopt 'mother' duties from about the age of 11. On top of the loss of her actual mother, she lost some of her childhood through this selfless action and probably received no recognition for it, no badge of honour or celebration of her contribution to her family or her resilience. 'Threats' looks at the ways our minds and bodies respond to these stresses and adversities. Miriam's body responds to the stresses of caring for a young child 24/7, money and feeling again the loss of her own mother. All this leads to continuous low-level stress hormones and sleep loss, which together leave her feeling fatigued and irritable. 'Meaning' is about the sense we make of these events and situations, and the assumptions and norms within any given society that influence our personal meanings. Part of the meaning Miriam makes of Mick's irritation at her daughter's crying is that, like her father, she might lose closeness to him, and eventually lose him, like she lost her mother and then closeness to her father, and was powerless to stop this happening. 'Threat responses' shows how many of the experiences that are often called 'symptoms' – such as low mood, panic, anxiety, and so on – can be understood as attempts to survive difficult situations in the past and present.

The four questions, with the addition of 'What are your resources and strengths?' helps to summarise what is known about the impact of damaging events and circumstances on the client's life. This in turn gives a clearer idea of the changes that may need to be made both individually and by others. An individual CBT approach might focus on Miriam's need to think more positively and combat her negative thoughts about the possibility of Mick leaving her, or being a bad mother. She might also be supported to plan to do some things she enjoys, or try to create small opportunities for herself and her partner to enjoy themselves together, or ways to bring her father back into the picture and regain what she values in her relationship with him. Indeed, these things might be helpful if they end up with Miriam feeling more positive and if the men in her life respond well and their relationships improve. But what if the men in her life are too preoccupied with their own problems to take much notice of Miriam? What if they think nothing needs to change. There might not be enough recognition of how Miriam, as a woman, is positioned by society as always the one who just gets on with it and who makes things better. She is the one feeling really low, but perhaps it is her partner and her father who really need to change, or perhaps it needs all of them to think differently so that Miriam receives the appreciation she deserves without having to be the one who pleads for it, a lone voice. Some therapies for severe mental health difficulties take an approach that includes the person's friends and family from the outset, such as Open Dialogue.[289] This avoids locating the problem in the person who is in most distress, but the members of the social network decide together, with the support of the therapists, how to understand what is happening and what to do. Open Dialogue is not currently widely available in the UK, but it has demonstrated very positive results and could become more available in future.

## SERVICES FOR MOTHERS WITH THEIR BABIES OR CHILDREN

The arrival of a baby brings changes in roles and relationships, interrupted sleep, new demands and often financial pressures. Many new parents feel stressed, especially those who don't have good support networks around them. Studies suggest that around 13 per cent of women and between 5 and 10 per cent of fathers[290] experience such low mood that they meet the criteria for a diagnosis of depression following childbirth.[291] Usually this resolves but for some it can be profound or prolonged. In this event, it can be particularly significant for mothers as it can have an enduring effect on both the mother's health and her child's development and affect her developing relationship with the baby.[292,293]

The approaches which can be helpful are the same as for depression at other times in life, but it is also important to consider and support the mother–baby relationship. There may be local groups available offering support to mothers of young children, for example in Children's Centres. As services vary from one area to another, the local health visitor or GP is usually a good source of information on what is available locally.

## HELP AT TIMES OF CRISIS

We may face many different types of crisis in our lives which can lead to depression or make recovery much harder. One person's idea of a crisis may be very different from someone else's. Often the crisis is of a social nature. We mention some issues below that are or can develop into a crisis and, in the resources section, we suggest resources and organisations which may be able to help with these difficulties.

Understanding depression

## HELP IN AN ABUSIVE SITUATION

When someone is in an abusive situation, it is important that they seek support to help them get to a safe space where they can think more clearly about what they want to do and get help. Some national charities and helplines are listed in the resources section of this document and there may be local services available. The police can offer help with immediate concerns and dangers and they may also be able to suggest local support.

There are now many forms of modern slavery which include sexual exploitation, domestic servitude, criminal exploitation and labour exploitation. Sadly, if this situation affects a person, their exploiters will make it difficult for them to access help or see how things could be different. If you are concerned that someone you know or come across is being exploited, you can contact the Modern Slavery helpline on 0800 121 700. Other contacts are listed in the resources section. Many of us can be complicit with modern slavery by using services which exploit people. We can all help by taking time to become more aware of the conditions people work in to provide us with goods and services.

Depending on the situation, there are a number of possible sources of help. There are links and contact details in the resources section of this report.

## RESPONDING TO A MENTAL HEALTH CRISIS

During a mental health crisis, the person experiencing the crisis requires urgent and immediate support, assistance and care from an emergency mental health service. There are many possible causes or triggers of crisis, and they may be psychological, physical or social. All crises will be different in their cause, prevention and progression. It is important to respond to individual, specific needs, while paying attention to surrounding circumstances.

There may be times when a person feels so low that they are at risk of harming themselves or others, directly or through neglect. This may also put them at risk of exploitation or abuse

by others. In these cases, they may need additional crisis support. Sometimes, the only help available is admission to an acute mental health ward, and whatever the circumstances this is likely to be difficult. Some people are sent to hospitals far away from their homes because local facilities are full. It can be difficult to stand up for your rights in these situations. It is useful to have the support of advocacy services[294], who will help to put the case to the correct people. Non-medical crisis houses offer an alternative to hospital and are very popular, but more are badly needed.[295]

## SELF-HARM

Some people harm themselves – for example cutting their arms – to try and cope with very difficult feelings. While of course it is distressing if someone close to you harms him or herself, it's important to understand why they are doing it, and to offer a kind, compassionate response rather than judgement. Current guidance recommends that, in addition to receiving good physical care for their injuries, people who self-harm should be offered an assessment of their psychological and social needs.[296]

## WAYS TO GET HELP IF YOU ARE FEELING VERY LOW OR SUICIDAL

Contact someone you trust, tell them how you feel, and talk through with them about what to do to get through the next few hours.

The Samaritans is a charity specialising in supporting people 24 hours a day who feel suicidal, and their national UK number is 116 123. You can find your local branch on their website.[297] There may also be a local suicide crisis helpline and/or house/café in your area.

The main sources of immediate help from the NHS for a suicidal crisis are accident and emergency departments and crisis support services provided by local mental health teams. Your GP will also try to help you if the surgery is open. There is always the national emergency number of 999.

## KNOWING YOUR RIGHTS

It's important at times of crisis to know your rights. Citizens' Advice provides information on a wide range of topics, including debt advice and your rights in various situations, and they can signpost to other people who can help.[298]

Mental health professionals are taught how to carry out a 'suicide risk assessment' by asking various questions. If the professional considers someone to be at immediate risk, they may feel hospital admission is necessary for the person's safety. However, if the person has the capacity to make the relevant decisions, it is their right in law that admission should first be offered on a voluntary basis. If admission to a psychiatric unit is something that you are certain you would never want for yourself or someone close, then it can be a good idea to document an 'advance decision'[299,300] about what you would like to happen (and not happen) in a crisis. It is worth looking into possible alternative provision locally and including that in the document. This may help to avoid the situation where if someone refuses admission but is felt to be at risk, they are admitted against their will. None the less, you do need to bear in mind that if your safety or that of others is at risk, your wishes can be overruled.

At the point of attempting suicide, a person is usually feeling utterly hopeless and believes there is no future and they would be better off dead. They may even feel that others will be better off without them. Sometimes someone who is suicidal might need a place in a crisis house, or even to be admitted to hospital. However, it is worth remembering that simple things may help the most, like someone listening and showing that they understand, including how the person has come to feel so hopeless about their future. Sitting with the person – perhaps on a rota – and enabling them to talk things through can make a huge difference.

> I've never forgotten the kindness of other patients when I was admitted to a therapeutic community – a hospital that's run like a big family with everyone helping each other with cooking and cleaning, and even setting up a rota when someone was suicidal. Someone was always there through the night.
>
> **Annie**

# Part 5: Prevention – Towards an anti-depressant society

# Part 5: Prevention – Towards an anti-depressant society

An ounce of prevention is worth a pound of cure.

**Benjamin Franklin**

## KEY POINTS

Prevention is vital – we need to address the underlying causes of depression rather than waiting until people are in crisis. This means addressing issues like poverty, violence, abuse, inequality, discrimination, social injustice, and the physical environment.

Enabling and supporting connections is one of the most important things we need to address in society. Connecting with others can provide support for people experiencing depression and prevent people from becoming depressed in the first place.

We need to create psychologically healthy communities, schools and work places.

We need to ensure that vulnerable people are supported within our communities, both practically and emotionally.

In Part 2, we identified some of the many complex, multi-layered and wide-ranging reasons that people become depressed. Addressing these issues is a global challenge.[301] Nevertheless, we can take action to make a difference.

In our view, depression is primarily a social rather than a brain problem: one that is related to the events and circumstances of our lives and the sense that we make of them. This means that our priority should be addressing problems in society that make it depressogenic, in other words, the things that make people more likely to become depressed.

## RESPONDING TO INEQUALITIES AND SOCIAL ISSUES

There is an ever-increasing gap between rich and poor.[302] As we highlighted in Part 2, there is no doubt that unequal societies are bad for our physical and mental health and austerity has had significant negative psychological effects for many.[303] It logically follows that a powerful, population-level way to improve our psychological wellbeing, and almost certainly to reduce depression, would be to reduce inequalities; we need to create a more equitable society.

As Richard Wilkinson and Kate Pickett put it in their popular book *The Spirit Level:*

'The solution to the problems caused by inequality is not more psychotherapy aimed at making everyone less vulnerable. The best way of responding to the harm done by high levels of inequality would be to reduce inequality itself.'[304]

There is also a need to proactively address important global issues, including climate change, which are inevitably linked to depression and other forms of emotional distress. Everyone can positively contribute to solutions by engaging with new social and political understandings and visions.[305] The Australian Psychological Society suggests strategies drawn from a review of relevant psychological knowledge to help people engage positively in the change we need.[306] These strategies include acknowledging the difficult feelings which we so often ignore or avoid, talking and raising awareness of environmental issues, and acting personally and collectively to contribute to solutions.

## MAKING CONNECTIONS

While local authorities and other government agencies have a key role in developing policies and facilities which help to create a more equitable society, we all have a part to play.

Making connections is probably the most important thing we need to think about as a society. As identified in Part 2, some of society's changes, including new technologies have not taken the importance of human connections into account. The importance of connecting with other humans and potentially with the emotional pain and suffering of another is a vital form of support for people experiencing depression. It can also prevent people from becoming depressed. This is not a new idea; many people from

different backgrounds and perspectives have recognised and talked about the importance of this.[307,308,309,310] The importance of making connections, tackling loneliness and reducing social isolation is clearly recognised by the UK government and is a key part of policy.[311,312,313] Ensuring that people are part of communities which recognise our interdependence and where different views can be voiced, heard and supported is an important part of creating the kind of society which encourages wellbeing.

A good example of a development which supported connections and enabled social change was a community psychology project with depressed women on the White City Estate in London.[314,315] At first, the women were offered individual psychotherapy, then they gathered in groups with other women and finally the groups supported each other to take action to change things in their social environment.

The box below gives a recent example of how a community is drawing on clinical psychologists with community psychology approaches to inform and support local people after the Grenfell Tower tragedy.

**Grenfell Tower**

The need for a unique response to this major incident affecting a whole community was quickly identified. The Grenfell Health and Wellbeing Service was set up and is trying to embed the values of community psychology into its work, focusing on empowerment, and placing people and problems in context. The service places a high priority on understanding and collaborating with the community and recognising complexity and cultural diversity. It works in partnership with local stakeholders, community organisations, and influential members of the community, and respects and uses local knowledge and networks. These relationships help to address barriers and develop more meaningful and relevant services. Working in this collaborative way, valuable groups have been created, for example, the Hand of Hope group for Arabic speaking women, a faith-informed bereavement group and Team of Life for young men. These groups have reached out to those affected by Grenfell who have not accessed more formal therapeutic support. Working together strengthens resilience and fosters a sense of ownership which means that community initiatives can continue when formal incident support is no longer available. This service is an example of how the NHS and communities can work together to provide support tailored for a particular context. [316]

## PSYCHOLOGICALLY HEALTHY ENVIRONMENTS AT SCHOOL

A recent UK parliamentary report into the role of education in children and young people's mental health found that schools and colleges have a 'frontline role in promoting and protecting children and young people's mental health and wellbeing'. [317]

School is where young people spend most of their time when not at home. As well as recognising and tackling problems early, a positive culture in the school community is vital to enable children to feel valued and to grow in confidence and ability. The leadership of the school needs to nurture both employees and pupils.

Bullying is a big issue and as described in Part 2, it often leads to later mental health problems. Schools therefore need not only to develop appropriate support for children who have been bullied but also links with relevant NHS mental health services. Perhaps even more importantly, schools should put in place robust systems to prevent bullying in the first place.

Various interventions in schools have been developed that could help children to grow up to have greater psychological wellbeing, rather than trying to help after things have gone wrong. [318] Establishing cultures which promote psychological safety and growth are vitally important and where these have been developed, for example in South East Wales, they are helping children, their families and staff across health, education and social care and ultimately whole communities. [319] However, culture change takes time and has to be developed locally.

New, psychologically informed service plans to promote mental health in schools are in an early stage of development in the UK but offer a real opportunity to change perceptions of mental health amongst children and teachers and promote psychologically healthy cultures. Further recommendations are discussed in detail in a recently published guide for professionals. [320]

# PSYCHOLOGICALLY HEALTHY ENVIRONMENTS AT WORK

The National Institute for Health and Clinical Excellence[321] (NICE) notes that work can be good for mental health in that it 'is an important determinant of self-esteem and identity' and 'can provide a sense of fulfilment and opportunities for social interaction'. In supporting the idea that work can have important benefits apart from providing income, the British Psychological Society report called *Psychology at Work*[322] makes the point that people should be encouraged into work by making it more attractive, rather than by making unemployment even more punitive.

The NICE guidance also notes that: 'Work can also have negative effects on mental health, particularly in the form of stress. Work-related stress is defined as "the adverse reaction people have to excessive pressure or other types of demand placed upon them".' So, good working conditions are important.

For England and the UK, recommendations include involving workers in decision-making and following Health and Safety Executive guidance for a work environment that minimises stress, promotes mental wellbeing, and enables flexible working as far as is practicable. NHS Health Scotland makes similar recommendations.[323]

*Thriving at Work*,[324] an independent review into how employers can better support mental health, revealed the huge human and financial cost of poor mental health at work. Refreshingly, the review started with the premise that mental health is an issue for all of us, and that we all fluctuate between thriving, struggling and suffering, sometimes to the extent of being off work. The review argues that we all need to be more aware of our own and others' mental health, and of how to cope when it fluctuates. Employers have a particular responsibility here, not only in providing good working conditions with a healthy work–life balance and opportunities for development, but also in improving mental health awareness among employees.

One of the most effective ways of making workplaces more healthy is involving employees in decisions and in designing their own jobs. The importance of this is made clear in a ten-year study of nearly five thousand workers[325] which showed that when workers were involved in planning their work, productivity increased and rates of sickness and depression halved.

For people at work who are depressed, sensitive practical and emotional support from employers can make all the difference.

## HOW TO HELP – LISTENING NOT LABELLING

When we or someone we know has difficulties, it can be difficult to know what to do, yet a few kind words can often make a huge difference. One thing that prevents people just stopping for a few minutes and asking someone (a work colleague or a student or pupil) how they are feeling, and listening to the answer, is the fear that they'll say the wrong thing. In schools, teachers can be the first to notice that a young person needs additional support. Simple, brief, training can help people feel confident in taking this simple first step.[326]

# A HUMANE WELFARE SYSTEM

The BPS *Psychology at Work* report mentioned above also makes the general point that current policies designed to encourage people back into work are based on a flawed understanding of human behaviour, meaning that they are not having the intended consequences. The BPS is working hard with other organisations to lobby the relevant bodies to review the current welfare system, particularly the Work Capability Assessment, and make it more informed and effective.

The problem with an episode of depression is that it can be cyclical: massive stress as a teacher meant that I was more than happy to give up my role in the workforce, move north and become, for the first time, full-time mother to our two children.

Depression, in amongst other things, struck after a number of years. That meant that my chance of re-joining the 'recognised' workforce gradually diminished as the years with no formal employment on my CV lengthened. A depressing thing to acknowledge.

An 'us and them' exists, I believe, even amongst those who claim to harbour no such distinction. After many years in the 'them' camp I can now be numbered as one of 'us' but it has taken far more unpaid hard work than most would allow themselves. I am not quite paying tax but next year should see me be required to do so; it will be an absolute pleasure and a sign that I am back!

**Fiona**

# Resources

## FIRST PERSON ACCOUNTS AND SERVICE USER/ SURVIVOR WEBSITES

www.madintheuk.com
Mad in the UK is a website about rethinking mental health practice in the UK and promoting positive change.

www.time-to-change.org.uk
Time to Change is a social movement that aims to promote growing awareness of the stigma that people experiencing mental health difficulties often face. Their online resources include personal stories as well as helpful advice on how we can best respond to our own mental distress, as well as that of others, often through the power of talking.

www.asylummagazine.org
'An international magazine for democratic psychiatry, psychology and community development.' Features articles written by service users, survivors and professionals.

www.madinamerica.com
A non-profit organisation highlighting service users' experiences and supporting alternatives to dominant mental health treatments.

www.mindfreedom.org
Mind Freedom aims to 'win human rights campaigns in mental health, challenge abuse by the psychiatric drug industry, support the self-determination of psychiatric survivors and mental health consumers and promote safe, humane and effective options in mental health'.

www.selfhelp.org.uk/home
Self Help Connect UK is the new national division of Self Help Nottingham and Nottinghamshire, an organisation which started in the 1980s. It now has about 30 years of experience of self-help and is a unique resource of expertise about how to establish and sustain self-help groups.

www.recoverydevon.co.uk
A website dedicated to promoting recovery methods and theories to help individuals make an informed decision about their recovery journey.

## MENTAL HEALTH ORGANISATIONS

www.mind.org.uk
MIND is a mental health charity which provides advice and support to empower anyone experiencing a mental health problem. They campaign to improve services, raise awareness and promote understanding. They also provide local services, such as crisis helplines, drop-in centres, counselling and befriending.

www.mentalhealth.org.uk
The Mental Health Foundation is a UK charity which provides information, carries out research and works to improve resources for people affected by mental health difficulties with a focus on recovery and wellbeing. Their online resources include articles and information about depression.

www.rethink.org
Rethink Mental Illness is a charity that focuses on quality of life for people affected by mental health issues. Their website includes helpful advice and information about depression.

www.mentalhealthrecovery.com/wrap-is/
Mary Ellen Copeland's website about recovery and the Wellness Recovery and Action Plan (WRAP) approach which is designed to enable people to negotiate with services to design a package of care that is most helpful for them, including plans for any crises. Includes links to resources.

www.compassionatemind.co.uk
The Compassionate Mind Foundation promotes an evolution and neuroscience informed

approach to compassion which now forms the basis of a psychotherapy (Compassion Focused Therapy) and Compassionate Mind Training. The last 10 years have seen an expanding evidence base for both the therapy and Compassionate Mind Training for the alleviation of mental health difficulties and promoting wellbeing.

www.rcpsych.ac.uk

The Royal College of Psychiatrists is the UK professional body for psychiatrists. The website has detailed information and resources for researchers, users of mental health services, the general public and the media.

www.researchintorecovery.com

This is a website about the work of the recovery research team with the Institute of Mental Health at the University of Nottingham. It contains many downloadable resources and information about research on recovery and wellbeing.

www.youngminds.org.uk

Young Minds is a UK charity committed to improving the emotional wellbeing and mental health of young people and empowering their parents and carers. Their website includes resources and information about depression, specifically aimed at informing young people and their families.

## PSYCHOLOGISTS' WEBSITES

www.bps.org.uk/public

Public information section of the British Psychological Society website, containing resources to help you learn about psychology, the work that psychologists do, and how to find a psychologist if you need support.

http://www.bps.org.uk/dcp

Website of the British Psychological Society Division of Clinical Psychology.

https://blogs.canterbury.ac.uk/discursive/

'Views and commentary on psychology, mental health and other stuff' from the Salomons Institute for Applied Psychology at Canterbury Christ Church University. A frequent theme is how we understand and respond to 'mental illness'.

www.peterkinderman.blogspot.co.uk

Clinical psychologist and contributor to this report Professor Peter Kinderman's blog. Deals with psychological models of mental health problems, and mental health policy.

www.rufusmay.com

Set up by clinical psychologist Rufus May, this website provides a resource of articles, interviews and other media that Rufus has taken part in, promoting a holistic, positive psychology approach to emotional health and recovery.

www.understandingdepression.net

Address for the website associated with this report.

## SELF-HELP SITES

https://www.nhs.uk/oneyou/every-mind-matters/

Online information with free tips, tools, support and encouragement to help manage and maintain mental health. You can take a quiz to see how you're doing now and create your own mind plan to help you make changes to fit your life and make you feel good. The site has been developed by Public Health England.

www.livinglifetothefull.com

This is an online life skills resource using CBT principles to help individuals with life difficulties using a cognitive behavioural approach.

www.moodgym.com.au
A free self-help programme to help people understand and use basic cognitive behavioural therapy techniques for depression and anxiety.

https://www.psychology.org.au/for-the-public/Psychology-topics/Climate-change-psychology/Coping-with-climate-change-distress
A resource developed by the Australian Psychological Society which focuses on responding to emotional distress related to climate change.

## OTHER USEFUL SITES

www.madintheuk.com
Mad in the UK promotes an alternative perspective to the current diagnostic approach to mental healthcare. They emphasise the role of social adversity to mental distress, and campaign for changes in the discourse around mental health.

www.cepuk.org
The Council for Evidence-Based Psychiatry communicates evidence of the harmful effects of psychiatric medications, particularly when these are taken long-term. They offer an alternative perspective to the mainstream 'medical' approach within psychiatry.

www.rxisk.org
RxISK is a free, independent medication safety website that aims to help people weigh up the benefits of medication alongside its potentially harmful side-effects.

www.studentagainstdepression.org
Students Against Depression offers advice, information and guidance to those affected by low mood, depression and suicidal thinking.

## SUPPORT IN TIMES OF CRISIS

www.samaritans.org
The Samaritans provide confidential, non-judgemental support, 24 hours every day of the year. They can be contacted about any issue, and support people to talk about what they are going through. Their free-phone number is 116 123.

https://www.mind.org.uk/information-support/legal-rights/
MIND have an extensive range of helpful resources available from their main website given on the first page of this resources section. This link directs you to the legal rights section which signpost to various information which could be helpful in a crisis. There is also a tool easily accessible from a tab on their website which you can use to guide you if you need urgent help.

www.moneyandmentalhealth.org
People with mental health problems are three and a half times as likely to be in problem debt. Money and Mental Health is an independent charity, committed to breaking the link between financial difficulty and mental health problems.

## HELP WHEN YOU ARE EXPERIENCING VIOLENCE, HARASSMENT OR ABUSE

www.refuge.org.uk
www.womensaid.org.uk
Refuge and Women's Aid provide advice and help for people experiencing abuse at home. They also work together to provide a 24-hour National Domestic Violence Helpline on 0808 2000 247.

www.mensadviceline.org.uk
www.mankind.org.uk
Men who are experiencing abuse or violence at home can call the Men's Advice Line free on 0808 801 1327 or Mankind on 01823 334 244.

www.karmanirvana.org.uk
www.gov.uk/guidance/forced-marriage
For forced marriage and 'honour' crimes, contact Karma Nirvana (0800 5999 247) or the Forced Marriage Unit (020 7008 0151).

www.stonewall.org.uk
www.galop.org.uk
Stonewall campaigns for equality for LGBT+ people and Galop is an LGBT+ anti-violence charity, which support people who have experienced hate crime, sexual violence or domestic abuse.

www.childline.org.uk
For children and young people, Childline offers free, confidential counselling through online and telephone support (0800 1111).

www.citizensadvice.org.uk
Citizens' Advice provides information on a wide range of topics including your rights in various situations, and they can signpost to people who can help.

www.modernslaveryhelpline.org
The Modern Slavery Helpline provides vital information and support for victims of slavery in the UK. Their free-phone number is 08000 121 700.

## REFERENCES

[1] World Health Organization (2017). Depression and Other Common Mental Health Disorders: Global Health Estimates. WHO/MSD/MER/2017.2 https://who.int/mental_health/management/depression/prevalence_global_health_estimates/en/

[2] https://changingmindsuk.com/wp-content/uploads/2019/03/Understanding-formulation.pdf

[3] Moussavi, S., Chatterji, S., Verdes, E. et al. (2007). Depression, chronic diseases, and decrements in health: results from the World Health Surveys. *Lancet, 370*, 851–858.

[4] World Health Organization (2017). Depression and Other Common Mental Health Disorders: Global Health Estimates. WHO/MSD/MER/2017.2 https://who.int/mental_health/management/depression/prevalence_global_health_estimates/en/

[5] World Health Organization (2017). Depression and Other Common Mental Health Disorders: Global Health Estimates. WHO/MSD/MER/2017.2 https://who.int/mental_health/management/depression/prevalence_global_health_estimates/en/

[6] Gudmundsen, GR, Rhew, I.C., McCauley, E., Kim, J. & Vander Stoep, A. (2019) Emergence of depressive symptoms from kindergarten to sixth grade. *Journal of Clinical Child & Adolescent Psychology, 48*(3), 501–515. doi:10.1080/15374416.2017.1410823

[7] Green, H., McGinnity, A., Meltzer, H. et al. (2005). *Mental health of children and young people in Great Britain*. London, HMSO. Available via http://www.esds.ac.uk/doc/5269/mrdoc/pdf/5269technicalreport.pdf

[8] Riihimaki, K., Vuorilehto, T., Melartin, J. et al. (2014). Incidence and predictors of suicide attempts among primary-care patients with depressive disorders: A 5-year prospective study. *Psychological Medicine, 44*(2), 291–302. https:// doi:10.1017/S0033291713000706

[9] Spijker, J., de Graaf, R., Ten Have, M. et al. (2010). Predictors of suicidality in depressive spectrum disorders in the general population: Results of the Netherlands Mental Health Survey and Incidence Study. *Social Psychiatry & Psychiatric Epidemiology, 45*(5), 513–521.

[10] Office for National Statistics. (2020). Retrieved 13 September 2020 from http://www.ons.gov.uk/peoplepopulationandcommunity/birthsdeathsandmarriages/deaths/datasets/suicidesintheunitedkingdomreferencetables

[11] Office for National Statistics. (2020). Retrieved 13 September 2020 from http://www.ons.gov.uk/peoplepopulationandcommunity/birthsdeathsandmarriages/deaths/datasets/suicidesintheunitedkingdomreferencetables

[12] https://www.samaritans.org/about-samaritans/research-policy/suicide-facts-and-figures/

[13] WHO (2014). Preventing suicide: A global imperative. https://www.who.int/mental_health/suicide-prevention/world_report_2014/en/

[14] http://cepuk.org/unrecognised-facts/no-biological-causes/

[15] https://joannamoncrieff.com/2014/05/01/the-chemical-imbalance-theory-of-depression-still-promoted-but-still-unfounded/

[16] https://www.madinamerica.com/2015/04/psychiatrists-still-promoting-low-serotonin-theory-depression/

[17] http://cepuk.org/unrecognised-facts/myth-of-the-chemical-imbalance/

[18] Harré, R. (1986). An outline of the social constructionist viewpoint. In R. Harré (Ed.) *The*

social construction of emotions, pp.2–14. Oxford: Basil Blackwell.

19 Hanninen, V. & Valkonen, J. (2019). *Losing and regaining grip: Depression and everyday life*. SAGE Open. January to March, pp.1–9, doi:10.1177/2158244018822371.

20 National Institute for Health and Care Excellence (2009). *Depression in adults – full guidance* [NICE CG90]. Retrieved October 2014 from http://www.nice.org.uk/guidance/cg90/chapter/guidance

21 Beck, A.T., Rush, A.J., Shaw, B.F. & Emery, G. (1987). *Cognitive therapy of depression*. New York: Guilford.

22 Gilbert, P. (2009). *Overcoming depression: A self-help guide using cognitive behavioural techniques*. London: Constable and Robinson.

23 Watts, F.N., MacLeod, A.K. & Morris, L. (2011). Associations between phenomenal and objective aspects of concentration problems in depressed patients. *British Journal of Psychology, 79*(2). doi:10.1111/j.2044-8295.1988.tb02285.x

24 Nolen-Hoeksema, S. (2000). The role of rumination in depressive disorders and mixed anxiety/depressive symptoms. *Journal of Abnormal Psychology, 109*(3), 504–511.

25 https://www.england.nhs.uk/wp-content/uploads/2017/09/practice-primer.pdf

26 Serby, M. & Yu, M. (2003). Overview: depression in the elderly. *Mount Sinai Journal of Medicine, 70*(1), 38–44.

27 Lisa A. Martin, PhD; HaroldW. Neighbors, PhD; Derek M. Griffith, PhD (2013). The Experience of Symptoms of Depression in Men vs Women Analysis of the National Comorbidity Survey Replication. *JAMA Psychiatry,* Volume 70, Number 10, 1100–1106. doi:10.1001/jamapsychiatry.2013.1985

28 Chentsova-Dutton, Y.E. & Tsai, J.L. (2010). Self-focused attention and emotional response: The role of culture. *Journal of Personality and Social Psychology, 98*, 507–519.

29 Lin, K-M. & Cheung, F. (1999). Medical health issues of Asian Americans. *Psychiatric Services, 50*(6), 774–780.

30 National Institute for Health and Care Excellence (2010). *Depression: The NICE guideline on the treatment of depression in adults* (Updated edn).

31 Time to Change, 2010. Retrieved 14 April 2014 from http://www.time-to-change.org.u/sites/default/files/imce_uploads/Family%20Matters.pdf

32 Inayat, Q. (2005). Islam, divinity and spiritual healing. In R. Moodley & D. West (Eds.) *Integrating traditional healing practices into counseling and psychotherapy*, (pp.159–169). Thousand Oaks, CA: Sage.

33 Golden, R.N., Gaynes, B.N., Ekstrom, R.D. et al. (2005). The efficacy of light therapy in the treatment of mood disorders: A review and meta-analysis of the evidence. *American Journal of Psychiatry, 162,* 656–662.

34 McCraw, S., Parker, G., Fletcher, K. & Friend, P. (2013). Self-reported creativity in bipolar disorder: Prevalence, types and associated outcomes in mania versus hypomania. *Journal of Affective Disorders, 151*(3), 831–836. doi:10.1016/j.jad.2013.07.016

35 British Psychological Society. (2010) *Understanding bipolar disorder*. Available via http://shop.bps.org.uk/understanding-bipolar-disorder.html

36 National Institute for Health and Care Excellence. (2009). *Depression in adults – Recognition and management* [NICE CG90]. Retrieved October from https://www.nice.org.uk/guidance/cg90

37 Division of Clinical Psychology (2014). *Understanding Psychosis and Schizophrenia: Why people sometimes hear voices, believe things that others find strange, or appear out of touch with reality, and what can help.* Leicester: British Psychological Society. https://www.bps.org.uk/sites/www.bps.org.uk/files/Page%20-%20Files/Understanding%20Psychosis%20and%20Schizophrenia.pdf

38 Herman, J. (1997). *Trauma and recovery*. New York: Basic Books.

39 Division of Clinical Psychology (2014). *Understanding Psychosis and Schizophrenia: Why people sometimes hear voices, believe things that others find strange, or appear out of touch with reality, and what can help.* Leicester: British Psychological Society. https://www.bps.org.uk/sites/www.bps.org.uk/files/Page%20-%20Files/Understanding%20Psychosis%20and%20Schizophrenia.pdf

40 Macmillan, D. (2015). *Every brilliant thing*. London: Oberon Modern Plays.

41 'Depression Symptoms, Causes, and Diagnosis.' National Alliance on Mental Illness. Web. 17 Feb. 2012. http://www.nami.org/Template.cfm?

42 Dohrenwend, B.S. & Dohrenwend, B.P. (1974). *Stressful life events*. New York: Wiley.

43 Wakefield, J.C. (2012). Mapping melancholia: the continuing typological challenge for major depression. *Journal of Affective Disorders, 138*, 180–182. doi:10.1016/j.jad.2011.02.013

44 Kendler, K.S. Hettema, J.M., Butera, F et al. (2003). Life event dimensions of loss, humiliation, entrapment, and danger in the prediction of onsets of major depression and generalized anxiety. *Arch Gen Psychiatry, 60*(8), 789–796. doi:10.1001/archpsyc.60.8.789

REFERENCES

45  McLeod, J.D. (1991). Childhood parental loss and adult depression. *Journal of Health and Social Behavior 32*(3), 205–220.

46  Brown, G.W. & Harris, T. (1978). *Social origins of depression: A study of psychiatric disorder in women.* New York: Free Press.

47  Oatley, K. & Bolton, W. (1985). A social-cognitive theory of depression in reaction to life events. *Psychological Review, 92*, 372–388.

48  Haslam, S.A. (2014). Making good theory practical: Five lessons for an applied social identity approach to challenges of organizational, health, and clinical psychology. *British Journal of Social Psychology, 53*, 1–20.

49  Butterworth, P., Leach, L.S., Strazdins, L. et al. (2011). The psychosocial quality of work determines whether employment has benefits for mental health: results from a longitudinal national household panel survey. *Occupational and Environmental Medicine, 68*, 806–812.

50  Cooklin, A.R., Canterford, L., Strazdins, L. & Nicholson, J.M. (2011). Employment conditions and maternal postpartum mental health: results from the longitudinal study of Australian children. *Archives of Women's Mental Health, 14*, 217–225.

51  Felitti, V.J., Anda, R.F., Nordenberg, D. et al. (1998). Relationship of childhood abuse and household dysfunction to many of the leading causes of death in adults: The Adverse Childhood Experiences (ACE) Study. *American Journal of Preventive Medicine, 14*(4), 245–258.

52  http://www.acestudy.org/index.html

53  https://www.scotphn.net/wp-content/uploads/2016/06/2016_05_26-ACE-Report-Final-AF.pdf

54  http://bccewh.bc.ca/wp-content/uploads/2012/05/2013_TIP-Guide.pdf

55  https://www.cdc.gov/violenceprevention/acestudy/index.html

56  Vibhakar, V., Allen, L.R., Gee, B. & Meiser-Stedman, R. (2019). A systematic review and meta-analysis on the prevalence of depression in children and adolescents after exposure to trauma. *Journal of Affective Disorders, 255*, 77–89.

57  Kendler, K.S., Bulik, C.M., Silberg, J. et al. (2000). Childhood sexual abuse and adult psychiatric and substance use disorders in women: an epidemiological and cotwin control analysis. *Archives of General Psychiatry 57*, 953–959.

58  Cong, E., Li, Y.C. & Shao, C. et al (2012). Childhood sexual abuse and the risk for recurrent major depression in Chinese women. *Psychological Medicine, 42*, 409–417. doi:10.1017/S0033291711001462

59  Schilling, E.A., Aseltine Jr, R.H. & Gore, S. (2007). Adverse childhood experiences and mental health in young adults: A longitudinal survey. *BMC Public Health,* 7:30. doi:10.1186/1471-2458-7-30

60  Jonas, S. Bebbington, P., McManus,S. et al. (2011). Sexual abuse and psychiatric disorder in England: Results from the 2007 Adult Psychiatric Morbidity Survey. *Psychological Medicine, 41*, 709–719. doi:10.1017/S003329171000111X

61  Mullen, P.E., Martin, J.L., Anderson, J.C., Romans S.E. & Herbison, G.P. (1993). Childhood sexual abuse and mental health in adult life. *Brit. J. Psychiatry, 163*, 721–32.

62  Gladstone, G.L., Parker, G.B., Mitchell, P.B. et al. (2004). Implications of childhood trauma for depressed women: An analysis of pathways from childhood sexual abuse to deliberate self-harm and revictimization. *Am J Psychiatry, 161*(8), 1417–25.

63  Easton, S.D., Renner, L.M. & O'Leary, P. (2013). Suicide attempts among men with histories of child sexual abuse: Examining abuse severity, mental health, and masculine norms. *Child Abuse and Neglect, 37*(6), *June 2013,* 380–387. doi:10.1016/j.chiabu.2012.11.007

64  Takizawa, R., Maughan, B. & Arseneault, L. (2014). Adult health outcomes of childhood bullying victimization: Evidence from a five-decade longitudinal British birth cohort. *American Journal of Psychiatry, Volume 171 Issue 7, July 2014,* 777–784. doi:10.1176/appi.ajp.2014.13101401

65  Van Noorden, M., Minkenberg, S., Giltay, E. et al. (2011). Pre-adult versus adult onset major depressive disorder in a naturalistic patient sample: The Leiden Routine Outcome Monitoring Study. *Psychological Medicine, 41*, 1407–1417.

66  Bowes, L., Joinson, C., Wolke, D. & Glyn, L, (2015) Peer victimisation during adolescence and its impact on depression in early adulthood. *BMJ, 350,* h2469;

67  Lereya, S.T., Copeland, W.E., Costello , E.J. & Wolke, D. (2015). Adult mental health consequences of peer bullying and maltreatment in childhood. *The Lancet Psychiatry, 2, 6,* 524–531.

68  Barboza, G.E. (2015). The association between school exclusion, delinquency and subtypes of cyber- and F2F-victimizations: Identifying and predicting risk profiles and subtypes using latent class analysis. *Child Abuse and Neglect, 39,* 109–122. doi:10.1016/j.chiabu.2014.08.007

69  Beck, A.T., Rush, A.J., Shaw, B.F. & Emery, G. (1987). *Cognitive therapy of depression.* New York: Guilford.

70  Gilbert, P. (2009). *Overcoming depression: A self-help guide using cognitive behavioural techniques.* London: Constable and Robinson.

71 La Flair, L.N., Bradshaw, C.P. & Campbell, J.C. (2012). Intimate partner violence/abuse and depressive symptoms among female health care workers: Longitudinal findings. *Women's Health Issues, 22*(1), e53–e59. Retrieved from http://www.sciencedirect.com/science/article/pii/S1049386711001654

72 Devries A., Watts, C., Yoshihama, M. et al. WHO Multi-Country Study Team (2011). Violence against women is strongly associated with suicide attempts: Evidence from the WHO multi-country study on women's health and domestic violence against women. *Social Science & Medicine, 73*, 79e86. doi:10.1016/j.socscimed.2011.05.006

73 Wieclaw, J., Agerbo, E., Mortensen, P.B. et al. (2006). Work related violence and threats and the risk of depression and stress disorders. *Journal of Epidemiology and Community Health, 60*, 771–775.

74 Demir, D., Rodwell, J. & Flower, R. (2013). Workplace bullying among allied health professionals: prevalence, causes and consequences. *Asia Pacific Journal of Human Resources, 51*, 92–405.

75 Audit Scotland (2012) *Health inequalities in Scotland.* Edinburgh: Author. http://www.auditscotland.gov.uk/docs/health/2012/nr_121213_health_inequalities.pdf

76 Griffiths, A.W, Wood, A.M., Maltby, J., Taylor, P.J. & Tai, S. (2014). The prospective role of defeat and entrapment in depression and anxiety: A 12-month longitudinal study. *Psychiatry Research 216*(1), 52–59. doi:10.1016/j.psychres.2014.01.037

77 Wilkinson, R. & Pickett, K. (2018). *The inner level: How more equal societies reduce stress, restore sanity and improve everyone's wellbeing.* London: Allen Lane.

78 https://www.ohchr.org/Documents/Issues/Development/RightsCrisis/E-2013-82_en.pdf

79 https://www.openaccessgovernment.org/marmot-review-2020/82939/

80 McGrath, L., Griffin, V. & Mundy, E. (2015). *Psychologists Against Austerity: The Psychological Impact of Austerity, a briefing paper.* https://repository.uel.ac.uk/item/856z6

81 Kendler, K.S., Hetterma, J.M., Butera, F., Gardner, C.O. & Prescott, C.A. (2003). *Life event dimensions of loss, humiliation, entrapment and danger in the prediction of onsets of major depression and generalised anxiety.*

82 McDonaugh, P. (2000). Job insecurity and health. *International Journal of Health Services, Volume 30, Number 3,* 453–476.

83 Llena-Nozal, A. (2009). The effect of work status and working conditions on mental health in four OECD countries. *National Institute Economic Review 209:1,* 72–87.

84 Green, F. (2015). Health effects of job insecurity. IZA World of Labor 2015: 212 doi: 10.15185/izawol.212 I

85 Marmot, M. (2010). *Fair society, healthy lives: The Marmot review.* http://www.instituteofhealthequity.org/resources-reports/fair-society-healthy-lives-the-marmot-review/fairsociety-healthy-lives-full-report-pdf.pdf

86 Audit Scotland (2012). *Health inequalities in Scotland.* Edinburgh: Author.

87 Freidl, L. (2009). *Mental health, resilience and inequalities.* Copenhagen: World Health Organization Regional Office for Europe.

88 Zimmerman, F.J., Christakis, D.A. & Vader Stoep, A. (2004). Tinker, tailor, soldier, patient: Work attributes and depression disparities among young adults. *Social Science and Medicine, 58,* 1889–1901. doi:10.1016/S0277-9536(03)00410-6

89 Butler, A.C. (2014). Poverty and adolescent depressive symptoms. *American Journal of Orthopsychiatry, Vol. 84,* No. 1, 82–94. doi:10.1037/h0098735

90 Tracy, M. Zimmerman, F.J., Galea, S., McCauley, E. & Vander Stoep, A. (2008). What explains the relation between family poverty and childhood depressive symptoms? *Journal of Psychiatric Research, 42,* 1163–1175. doi:10.1016/j.jpsychires.2008.01.011

91 The impact of housing problems on mental health (2017). Shelter.org.uk. ComRes, Shelter.

92 Woolgar, M. & Tranah, T. (2010). Cognitive vulnerability to depression in young people in secure accommodation: The influence of ethnicity and current suicidal ideation. *Journal of Adolescence, 33,* 653–661. doi:10.1016/j.adolescence.2009.11.005

93 Schnittker, J., Massoglia, M. & Uggen, C. (2012). Out and down: Incarceration and psychiatric disorders. *Journal of Health and Social Behavior, 53*(4), 448–464. doi: 10.1177/0022146512453928

94 National Institute for Health and Care Excellence (2009). *Depression in adults with a chronic physical health condition: Recognition and management* [NICE CG91]. Retrieved from https://www.nice.org.uk/guidance/cg91/resources/depression-in-adults-witha-chronic-physical-health-problem-recognition-and-management-pdf-975744316357

95 Moussavi, S., Chatterji, S., Verdes, E., Tandon, A., Patel, V. & Ustun, B. (2007). Depression, chronic diseases, and decrements in health: results from the World Health Surveys. *Lancet, 370,* 851–858.

96 National Institute for Health and Care Excellence (2010). *Depression in Adults with Chronic Physical Health Problems: The NICE Guideline on Treatment and Management.*

97 UK Department of Health (2000). *No secrets: Guidance on developing and implementing multi-agency policies and procedures to protect vulnerable*

*adults from abuse.* Retrieved from https://www.gov.uk/government/uploads/system/uploads/attachment_data/file/194272/No_secrets__guidance_on_developing_and_implementing_multiagency_policies_and_procedures_to_protect_vulnerable_adults_from_abuse.pdf

[98]  Richards, D. (2011). Prevalence and clinical course of depression: A review. *Clinical Psychology Review, 31,* 1117–1125. doi:10.1016/j.cpr.2011.07.004

[99]  Lisa A. Martin, PhD; HaroldW. Neighbors, PhD; Derek M. Griffith, PhD (2013). The Experience of Symptoms of Depression in Men vs Women Analysis of the National Comorbidity Survey Replication. *JAMA Psychiatry, Volume 70, Number 10,* 1100–1106. doi:10.1001/jamapsychiatry.2013.1985

[100]  Office for National Statistics. (2018). Domestic abuse. London: Author. https://www.ons.gov.uk/peoplepopulationandcommunity/crimeandjustice/bulletins/domesticabuseinengland andwales/yearendingmarch2018#prevalence-of-domestic-abuse

[101]  Cheasty, M., Clare, A.W. & Collins. (1998). Relation between sexual abuse in childhood and adult depression: case-control study. *BMJ*; 316 :198.

[102]  De Vries, K.M., Mak, J.Y, Bacchus, L.J. et al. (2013). https://journals.plos.org/plosmedicine/article?id=10.1371/journal.pmed.1001439

[103]  Beydoun, H.A, Beydoun, M.A., Kaufman, J.S., Lo, B. & Zonderman, A.B. (2012). Intimate partner violence against adult women and its association with major depressive disorder, depressive symptoms and postpartum depression: A systematic review and meta-analysis. *Social Science and Medicine, 75,* 959–975. doi:10.1016/j.socscimed.2012.04.025

[104]  Ludermir, A.B., Lewis, G, Valongueiro, S.J., de Araujo, T.V.B. & Araya, R. (2010). Violence against women by their intimate partner during pregnancy and postnatal depression: A prospective cohort study. *Lancet,* 376, -910. doi:10.1016/S0140-6736(10)60887-2

[105]  Saunders, B.E., Villeponteaux, L.A., Lipovsky, J.A. et al. (1992). Child sexual assault as a risk factor for mental disorders among women. *Journal of Interpersonal Violence, 7,* 189–204.

[106]  Ussher, J.M. (1991). *Women's madness: Misogyny or mental illness?* New York: Harvester Wheatsheaf.

[107]  Marmot, 2010 Fair Society, healthy lives: The Marmot Review http://www.instituteofhealthequity.org/resources-reports/fair-society-healthy-lives-the-marmot-review/fairsociety-healthy-lives-full-report-pdf.pdf

[108]  McManus, S., Bebbington, P., Jenkins, R. & Brugha, T. (Eds.) (2016). Mental health and wellbeing in England: Adult Psychiatric Morbidity Survey 2014. Leeds: NHS Digital. Available at: http://content.digital.nhs.uk/catalogue/PUB21748/apms-2014-full-rpt.pdf

[109]  Call, J.B. & Shafer, K. (2018). Gendered manifestations of depression and help seeking among men. *American Journal of Men's Health, 12,* 41–51. doi:10.1177/1557988315623993

[110]  Cruwys, T., Dingle, G., Haslam, S.A. et al. (2013). Social group memberships protect against future depression, alleviate depression symptoms, and prevent depression relapse. *Social Science and Medicine, 98,* 179–186.

[111]  Missimme, S. & Bracke, P. (2010). Depressive symptoms among immigrants and ethnic minorities: a population-based study in 23 European countries. *Social Psychiatry and Psychiatric Epidemiology, 47*(1), 97–109.

[112]  Marshal, M.P., Dietz, L.J., Friedman, M.S. et al. (2011). Suicidality and depression disparities between sexual minority and heterosexual youth: A meta-analytic review. *Journal of Adolescent Health, 49,* 115–123.

[113]  http://www.liverpoolmentalhealth.org/_wp/wp-content/uploads/2012/11/Impact-of-Austerity-onWomens-Wellbeing-LMHC-Sept-2014.pdf

[114]  Bender, W.N., Rosenkrans, C.B. & Crane, M-K. (1999). Stress, depression and suicide among students with learning disabilities: Assessing the risk. *Learning Disabilities Quarterly, 22*(2), 143–156.

[115]  McDermott, S., Moran, R., Platt, T. et al. (2005). Depression in adults with disabilities, in primary care. *Disability and Rehabilitation, 27*(3), 117–123.

[116]  Richards, D. (2011). Prevalence and clinical course of depression: A review. *Clinical Psychology Review, 31,* -1125. doi:10.1016/j.cpr.2011.07.004

[117]  Nelson, G. & Prilleltensky, I. (2010). *Community psychology: In pursuit of liberation and wellbeing* (2nd edn). Basingstoke: Palgrave Macmillan.

[118]  Wright, E.R., Gronfein, W.P. & Owens, T.J. (2000). Deinstitutionalization, social rejection, and the selfesteem of former mental patients. *Journal of Health and Social Behavior, 41*(1), 68–90.

[119]  Brown, G.W. & Harris, T. (1978). *Social origins of depression: A study of psychiatric disorder in women.* New York: Free Press.

[120]  Myers, H.F., Wyatt, G.E., Ullman, J.B. et al. (2016). Cumulative burden of lifetime adversities: trauma and mental health in low-SES African Americans and latino/as. *Psychological Trauma: Theory, Research, Practice and Policy, Vol. 7 No. 3,* 243–51.

[121]  Harré, R. (2012). Positioning theory: Moral dimensions of social-cultural psychology. In J. Valsiner (Ed.) *The Oxford handbook of culture and psychology.* doi:10.1093/oxfordhb/9780195396430.013.0010

122 Foucault, M. (2001). *Madness and civilization: A history of insanity in the age of reason*. London: Routlege. First published in French in 1964.

123 Nelson, G. & Prilleltensky, I. (2010). *Community psychology: In pursuit of liberation and wellbeing* (2nd edn). Basingstoke: Palgrave Macmillan.

124 Berry, J.W. (2002). A psychology of immigration. *Journal of Social Issues*. https://doi.org/10.1111/0022-4537.00231

125 Hwang, W.C. & Myers, H.F. (2007). Major depression in Chinese Americans: The roles of stress and vulnerability. *Soc Psychiatr Psychiatr Epidemiol, 42*:189–197. [PubMed]

126 Obradovich, N., Migliorini, R., Paulus, M.P. & Rahwan, I. (2018). Empirical evidence of mental health risks posed by climate change. Proceedings of the National Academy of Sciences Oct 2018, 115 (43) 10953-10958. doi:10.1073/pnas.1801528115

127 Andrews, N. (2018). Conflicted about emotions: Ecological grief, love and truth. Green House Think Tank. https://www.greenhousethinktank.org/uploads/4/8/3/2/48324387/conflicted_about_emotions_n.andrews_gas.pdf

128 Bowlby, J. (1958). The nature of the child's tie to his mother. *International Journal of Psychoanalysis, 39,* 123.

129 Ainsworth, M.D.S., Blehar, M.C., Waters, E. & Wall, S. (1978). *Patterns of attachment: A psychological study of the strange situation*. Hillsdale, NJ: Erlbaum.

130 Schore, J.R. & Schore, A.N. (2014). *Regulation theory and affect regulation psychotherapy: A clinical primer, Smith College studies in social work, 84:2-3,* 178–195. doi:10.1080/00377317.2014.923719

131 Dallos, R. & Comley-Ross, P. (2005). Young people's experience of mentoring: building trust and attachments. *Clinical Child Psychology and Psychiatry, 10,* 369–383. doi:10.1177/1359104505053755

132 Beck, A.T. (1967). *Depression: Clinical, experimental and theoretical aspects* (reprinted 1972). New York: Harper and Row.

133 Beck, A.T., Rush, A.J., Shaw, B.F. & Emery, G. (1987). *Cognitive therapy of depression*. New York: Guilford.

134 Young, J.E., Klosko, J.S & Weishaar, M.E. (2003). *Schema therapy: A practitioner's guide*. New York: Guilford Press.

135 Dweck, C. (2017). *Mindset: Changing the way you think to fulfil your potential*. New York: Ballantine.

136 Labonte, B., Suderman, M., Maussion, G. et al. (2012). Genome-wide epigenetic regulation by early-life trauma. *Arch. Gen. Psychiatry 69,* 722–731.

137 Dar-Nimrod, I. & Heine, S.J. (2011). Genetic essentialism: On the deceptive determination of DNA. *Psychological Bulletin, Vol. 137,* 800–818.

138 Sloman, L. (2008). A new comprehensive evolutionary model of depression and anxiety. *Journal of Affective Disorders, 106,* 219–228.

139 Panksepp, J. (1998). *Affective neuroscience: The foundations of human and animal emotions*. Oxford: Oxford University Press.

140 Sloman, L. (2008). A new comprehensive evolutionary model of depression and anxiety. *Journal of Affective Disorders, 106,* 219–228.

141 Higgins, E.T. (1998). Promotion and prevention: Regulatory focus as a motivational principle. *Advances in Experimental Social Psychology, 30,* 1–46.

142 Barlow, D.H. (2000). *Anxiety and its disorders: The nature and treatment of anxiety and panic*. New York: Guilford.

143 Gilbert, P. (2013). *The compassionate mind*. London: Constable.

144 Allen, J.G. & Fonagy, P. (2006). *The handbook of mentalization-based treatment*. Chichester: Wiley.

145 Gonzalez, A. (2013). The impact of childhood maltreatment on biological systems: Implications for clinical interventions. *Paediatrics & Child Health, 18*(8), 415–418.

146 Miller, G.E. & Cole, S.W. (2012). Clustering of depression and inflammation in adolescents previously exposed to childhood adversity. *Biological Psychiatry, 72,* 34–40. doi:10.1016/j.biopsych.2012.02.034

147 Mohammadi, D. (2015). Brain under siege. *New Scientist, 226*(3027), 38–41.

148 Raison, C.L., Rutherford, R.E., Woolwine, B.J. et al. (2013). A randomized controlled trial of the tumor necrosis factor antagonist Infliximab for treatment-resistant depression: The role of baseline inflammatory biomarkers. *JAMA Psychiatry, 70,* 31–41. doi:10.1001/2013.jamapsychiatry.4.

149 http://www.zenithpharmabd.com/en/about/what-we-do/biomedicines/depression.html

150 https://joannamoncrieff.com/2014/05/01/the-chemical-imbalance-theory-of-depression-still-promotedbut-still-unfounded/

151 https://www.madinamerica.com/2015/04/psychiatrists-still-promoting-low-serotonin-theory-depression/

152 http://cepuk.org/unrecognised-facts/myth-of-the-chemical-imbalance/

153 Jacobs, B.L. (2004). Depression: The brain finally gets into the act. *Current Directions in Psychological Science, 13,* 103–106.

REFERENCES

154 Eisch, A.J. & Petrik, D. (2012). Depression and hippocampal neurogenesis: A road to remission? *Science, 338*, 72–75.

155 Dubovsky, S.L., Davies, R. & Dubovsky, A.N. (2001). Mood disorders. In R.E. Hales & S.C. Yudovsky (Eds.) *Textbook of clinical psychiatry*. Washington, DC: American Psychiatric Association.

156 LeDoux, J. (2002). *Synaptic self: How our brains become who we are*. London: Penguin.

157 Danese, A., Moffitt, T.E., Harrington, H. et al. (2009). childhood experiences and adult risk factors for age-related disease: depression, inflammation and clustering of metabolic risk markers. *Arch Pediatr Adolesc Med., 163*(12):1135. doi:10.1001/archpediatrics.2009.214

158 Brièrea, F.N., Rohdec, P., Seeleyc, J.R., Kleind, D. & Lewinsohn, P.M. (2014). Comorbidity between major depression and alcohol use disorder from adolescence to adulthood. *Comprehensive Psychiatry 55*, 526–533.

159 Carrigan, M.H. & Randall, C.L. (2003). Self-medication in social phobia: A review of the alcohol literature. *Addict Behav 28,* 269–284

160 Koob, G.F. & Le Moal, M. (2005). Plasticity of reward neurocircuitry and the 'dark side 'of drug addiction. *Nature Neuroscience, 8*(11), 1442–1444.

161 Mcintosh, C. & Ritson, B. (2001). Treating depression in substance misuse. *Advances in Psychiatric Treatment vol 7*, 357–364.

162 Hibblen, J.R. (1998). Fish consumption and major depression. *Lancet, 351*, 1213.

163 Holford, P. (2007). *Optimum nutrition for the mind*. London: Piatkus.

164 Nemets et al. (2002). Addition of omega-3 fatty acid to maintenance medication treatment for recurrent unipolar depressive disorder. *American Journal of Psychiatry, 159*, 477–479.

165 Raeder, M.B. et al. (2006). Associations between cod liver oil use and symptoms of depression: The Hordaland Health Study. *Journal of Affective Disorders, 101*, 245–249.

166 Taylor, M.J. et al. (2004). Folate for depressive disorders: Systematic review and meta-analysis of randomized control trials. *Journal of Psychopharmacology, 18*(2), 251–256.

167 Lomagno, K.A., Hu, F., Riddell, L.J. et al. (2014). Increasing iron and zinc in pre-menopausal women and its effect on mood and cognition: A systematic review. *Nutrients, 6*, 5117–5141. doi:10.3390/nu6115117

168 Golden, R.N., Gaynes, B.N., Ekstrom, R.D. et al. (2005). The efficacy of light therapy in the treatment of mood disorders: A review and meta-analysis of the evidence. *American Journal of Psychiatry, 162,* 656–662.

169 Zhai, L., Zhang, Y. & Zhang, D. (2015). Sedentary behaviour and the risk of depression: A meta-analysis. *British Journal of Sports Medicine, 49*, 705–709. doi:10.1136/bjsports-2014-093613

170 Gergen, K.J. (1991). *The saturated self*. New York: Basic Books.

171 Ehrenberg, A. (2009). *The weariness of the self: Diagnosing the history of depression in the contemporary age*. New York: McGill Press.

172 Wilkinson, R.G. & Pickett, K. (2010). *The spirit level: Why greater equality makes societies stronger*. New York: Bloomsbury Press.

173 Wilkinson, R.G. & Pickett, K. (2018). *The inner level: How more equal societies reduce stress, restore sanity and improve everyone's wellbeing*. London: Penguin Random House.

174 Cipriani et al. (2018). Comparative efficacy and acceptability of 21 antidepressant drugs for the acute treatment of adults with major depressive disorder: a systematic review and network meta-analysis. https://www.thelancet.com/journals/lancet/article/PIIS0140-6736(17)32802-7

175 Moncrieff, J. (2007). *The myth of the chemical cure*. Palgrave: Macmillan.

176 http://cepuk.org/unrecognised-facts/altered-mental-states/

177 Moncrieff, J. & Cohen, D. (2006). Do antidepressants cure or create abnormal brain states? http://journals.plos.org/plosmedicine/article?id=10.1371/journal.pmed.0030240

178 https://joannamoncrieff.com/2014/03/11/neutralising-suffering-how-the-medicalisation-of-distress-obliterates-meaning-and-creates-profit/

179 Moncrieff, J. (2013). *The bitterest pills*. Basingstoke: Palgrave Macmillan.

180 http://www.pulsetoday.co.uk/news/clinical-news/government-launches-major-review-into-prescription-drug-addiction/20036034.article

181 https://www.gov.uk/government/news/prescribed-medicines-that-may-cause-dependence-or-withdrawal

182 National Institute for Health and Care Excellence [NICE CG90] https://www.guidelines.co.uk/NICE/Depression/209641.article

183 National Institute for Health and Care Excellence (2019). *Depression in children and young people: Identification and management* [NICE NG 134].

184 Werneke, U., Northey, S. & Bhugra, D. (2006). Antidepressants and sexual dysfunction. doi:10.1111/j.16000447.2006.00890.x

185 *J Clin Psychiatry*. 2001;62 Suppl 3:10–21. Incidence of sexual dysfunction associated with antidepressant agents: a prospective multicenter study of 1022

outpatients. Spanish Working Group for the Study of Psychotropic-Related Sexual Dysfunction.

[186] Fournier, J.C. DeRubeis, R.J., Hollon, S.D. et al. (2010). Antidepressant drug effects and depression severity a patient-level meta-analysis. *JAMA, 303*(1), 47–53. doi:10.1001/jama.2009.1943

[187] Peter Goetsche antidepressants do more harm than good: http://www.thelancet.com/journals/lanpsy/article/PIIS2215-0366(14)70280-

[188] http://www.mind.org.uk/information-support/drugs-and-treatments/antidepressants/#.V_-Oo4WcFPY or http://www.mind.org.uk/media/1672916/making-sense-of-antidepressants_2014_pdf.pdf

[189] https://rxisk.org/

[190] http://www.mind.org.uk/information-support/drugs-and-treatments/antidepressants/#.V_-Oo4WcFPY or http://www.mind.org.uk/media/1672916/making-sense-of-antidepressants_2014_pdf.pdf

[191] Wainright, T. (2011). Psychologists and electroconvulsive therapy. *Clinical Psychology Forum, 271*, 28–30. https://www.yumpu.com/en/document/view/54504053/clinical-psychology-forum/33

[192] British Psychological Society (2007). Memorandum Submitted by the British Psychological Society (MH 6). London: Hansard. http://www.publications.parliament.uk/pa/cm200607/cmpublic/mental/memos/uc602.htm

[193] Electroconvulsive therapy: survey covering the period from January 2002 to March 2002. *Statistical Bulletin 2003/08*. Department of Health.

[194] National Institute for Health and Care Excellence (2010). *Depression in children and young people: identification and management* [NICE NG 134].

[195] Read, J., Harrop, C., Geekie, J. & Renton, J. (2018). An audit of ECT in England 2011-2015: Usage, demographics, and adherence to guidelines and legislation. *Psychol Psychother, 91*(3), 263–277. doi:10.1111/papt.12160. Epub 2017 Oct 20. https://www.ncbi.nlm.nih.gov/pubmed/29052308

[196] National Institute for Health and Care Excellence (2010). *Depression in adults – Recognition and management* (Updated edn) [NICE CG 90]. Retrieved October from https://www.nice.org.uk/guidance/cg90

[197] National Institute for Health and Care Excellence (2019). *Depression in children and young people: identification and management* [NICE CG 134]. https://www.nice.org.uk/guidance/ng134/chapter/Update-information.

[198] Bob, service user. *MIND Membership News, Winter 2015*, p.22.

[199] Rasmussen, K. (2009) Sham electroconvulsive therapy studies in depressive illness: A review of the literature and consideration of the placebo phenomenon

[200] in electroconvulsive therapy practice. *Journal of ECT, 25*, 54–59.

[201] Read, J. & Bentall, R. (2010). The effectiveness of electroconvulsive therapy: A literature review. *Epidemilogia e Psichiatria Sociale, 19*(4).

[201] Rogers, A. Pilgrim, D. & Lacey, R. (1993). *Experiencing psychiatry: Users' views of services*. London: Macmillan/ MIND.

[202] MIND (2001). Shock Treatment: A survey of people's experiences of Electro-Convulsive Therapy. www.ect.org/wp-content/uploads/2006/07/UK Mind report survey.doc

[203] National Institute for Health and Care Excellence (2009). *Depression in adults – Recognition and management* [NICE CG 90]. Retrieved October from https://www.nice.org.uk/guidance/cg90

[204] https://www.scie.org.uk/co-production/

[205] https://www.selfhelp.org.uk/directory/entry/mind-medication-and-wellbeing-group-nottingham

[206] Coles, S.K. & Diamond, B. (Eds.) (2013). *Madness contested: Power and practice* (pp.56–73). Ross-on-Wye: PCCS Books.

[207] http://www.lslcs.org.uk/

[208] Venner, F. & Noad, M. (2013). Beacon of hope. In S. Coles, S. Keenan & B. Diamond (Eds.) *Madness contested; Power and practice*. Monmouth: PCCS Books.

[209] http://www.lslcs.org.uk/wp-content/uploads/Summary-report-final_May12.pdf

[210] https://www.england.nhs.uk/mental-health/case-studies/aldershot/

[211] https://www.manchestermind.org/our-services/young-people/yasp/internet-cafe/

[212] https://www.theguardian.com/social-care-network/2013/aug/19/cafe-young-people-mental-healthsupport

[213] https://www.healthcareconferencesuk.co.uk/news/newsfiles/charter-2016_1314.pdf

[214] Ballatt, J. & Campling, P. (2011). *Intelligent kindness: Reforming the culture of healthcare*. London: RCPsych Publications.

[215] https://www.bmj.com/bmj/section-pdf/187887?path=/bmj/346/7907/Head_to_Head.full.pdf

[216] Smail, D. (2001). *Why therapy doesn't work*. London: Robinson.

[217] https://www1.bps.org.uk/system/files/Public%20files/cpf_david_smail_feb_2015.pdf

[218] https://www.scottishrecovery.net/

[219] https://www.ncbi.nlm.nih.gov/pubmed/28942748

[220] https://www.ncbi.nlm.nih.gov/pmc/articles/PMC3796297/

221 https://www.mentalhealth.org.uk/sites/default/files/Feeding-Minds.pdf

222 https://www.mind.org.uk/information-support/types-of-mental-health-problems/sleep-problems/about-sleep-and-mental-health

223 https://www.mentalhealth.org.uk/sites/default/files/MHF-Sleep-Report-2011.pdf)

224 National Institute for Health and Care Excellence (2009). *Depression in adults – Recognition and management* [NICE CG90]. Retrieved October from https://www.nice.org.uk/guidance/cg90

225 Knapen, J., Vancampfort, D., Moriën, Y. & Marchal, Y. (2015). Exercise therapy improves both mental and physical health in patients with major depression. *Disability and Rehabilitation, 37*(16), 1490–1495. doi:10.3109/09638288.2014.972579

226 Daley, A.J., Blamey, R.V., Jolly, K. et al. (2015). A pragmatic randomized controlled trial to evaluate the effectiveness of a facilitated exercise intervention as a treatment for postnatal depression: The PAM PeRS trial. *Psychological Medicine, 45*, 2413–2425. doi:10.1017/S0033291715000409

227 https://www.mindful.org/jon-kabat-zinn-defining-mindfulness

228 Pilkington, K., Kirkwood, G., Rampes, H. & Richardson, J. (2005). Yoga for depression: The research evidence. *Journal of Affective Disorders, 89,* 13–24. doi:10.1016/j.jad.2005.08.013 https://www.sciencedirect.com/science/article/pii/S0165032705002570?via%3Dihub

229 Mental Health Foundation (2000). *Strategies for living.* London: Author. https://www.mentalhealth.org.uk/sites/default/files/strategies_for_living_summary.pdf

230 Cruwys, T., South, E.I., Greenaway, K.H. & Haslam, S.A. (2015). Social identity reduces depression by fostering positive attributions. *Social Psychological and Personality Science, 6*, 65–74.

231 Leamy, M., Bird, V., Le Boutillier, C., Williams, J. & Slade, M. (2011). Conceptual framework for personal recovery in mental health: Systematic review and narrative synthesis. *British Journal of Psychiatry, 199*, 445–452. doi:10.1192/bjp.bp.110.083733

232 Wong, Y-L. I., Stanton, M.C. & Sands, R.G. (2014). Rethinking social inclusion: Experiences of persons in recovery from mental illness. *American Journal of Orthopsychiatry, 84*, 685–695. doi:10.1037/ort0000034.

233 Priestley, J., McPherson, S.J. & Davies, F. (2018). Couples disease: The experience of living with a partner with chronic depression. *Journal of Couple and Relationship Therapy, 17*(2), 128–145. doi:10.1080/15332691.2017.1372833

234 Gilbert, P. (2013). *The compassionate mind.* London: Robinson.

235 Mind http://www.mind.org.uk/

236 The Carers Trust. (2013). *The triangle of care carers included: A guide to best practice in mental health care in England* (2nd edn). London: Carers Trust. Available via http://static.carers.org/files/toc-professionals-2-11--2-6498.docxhttp://static.carers.org/files/the-triangle-of-care-carers-included-final-6748.pdf

237 Priestley, J. & McPherson, S. (2016). Experiences of adults providing care to a partner or relative with depression: A meta-ethnographic synthesis. *Journal of Affective Disorders, 192*, 41–49. doi:10.1016/j.jad.2015.12.011

238 Clement, S. et al. (2015) What is the impact of mental health-related stigma on help-seeking? A systematic review of quantitative and qualitative studies. *Psychol Med, 45*(1), 11–27. doi:10.1017/S0033291714000129. Epub 2014 Feb 26.

239 Depression: The Treatment and Management of Depression in Adults (Updated Edition). NICE Clinical Guidelines, No. 90.https://www.ncbi.nlm.nih.gov/books/NBK63772/

240 National Institute for Health and Care Excellence *Depression: The Treatment and Management of Depression in Adults* (Updated Edition) [NICE CG 90]. https://www.ncbi.nlm.nih.gov/books/NBK63772/

241 Lu, L. & Yuen, F. (2012). Journey women: Art therapy in a decolonizing framework of practice. *The Arts in Psychotherapy, 39*, 192–200.

242 Margrove, K.L., South Essex Service User Research Group [SE-SURG], Heydinrich, K. & Secker J. (2013). Waiting list-controlled evaluation of a participatory arts course for people experiencing mental health problems. *Perspectives in Public Health, 133*(1), 28–35.

243 Moxley, D.P., Feen-Calligan, H.R., Washington, O.G.M., & Garriott, L. (2011). Quilting in self-efficacy group work with older African American women leaving homelessness. *Art Therapy: Journal of the American Art Therapy Association, 28*(3), 113–122.

244 Stevens, J., Butterfield, C., Whittington, A. & Holttum, S. (2018). Evaluation of arts based courses within a UK recovery college for people with mental health challenges. *International Journal of Environmental Research and Public Health, 15*(6), 1170. doi:10.3390/ijerph15061170

245 Coulton, S., Clift, S., Skingley, A. & Rodriguez, J. (2015). Effectiveness and cost-effectiveness of community singing on mental health-related quality of life of older people: randomised controlled trial. *British Journal of Psychiatry, 207*(3), 250–5. https://www.artshealthandwellbeing.org.uk/sites/default/files/Coultonetal2015Singingandolderpeople RCT.pdf

246 Gilbert, P. (2013). *The compassionate mind.* London: Robinson.

247 Brogan, C. (2018). Donald Winnicott's unique view of depression with particular reference to his 1963 paper on the value of depression. *British Journal of Psychotherapy, 34*(3), 358–375.

248 Cantopher, T. (2003). *Depressive illness: The curse of the strong.* London: Sheldon Press.

249 Gut, E. (1989). *Productive & unproductive depression: Success or failure of a vital process.* London: Routledge.

250 Davies, J. (2012). The importance of suffering: The value and meaning of emotional discontent. London: Routledge.

251 Razzaque, R. (2014). *Breaking down is waking up: Can psychological suffering be a spiritual gateway?* London: Watkins.

252 https://spiritualcrisisnetwork.org.uk

253 Hurtado, G., Morales, L.R.A., Seligman, L.D. (2014). Religion-based emotional social support mediates the relationship between intrinsic religiosity and mental health. *Archives of Suicide Research,18*(4),376–391.

254 Disability Rights UK. (2012). Retrieved 25 October 2015 from http://www.disabilityrightsuk.org/

255 Chartered Institute of Personnel and Development (2015). Harassment and bullying at work. Retrieved 25 October 2015 from http://www.cipd.co.uk/hr-resources/factsheets/harassment-bullying-at-work.aspx

256 Disability Rights UK. (2012). Retrieved 25 October 2015 from http://www.disabilityrightsuk.org/

257 The Equality Act. (2010). Retrieved 25 October 2015 from http://www.legislation.gov.uk/ukpga/2010/15/contents

258 Chartered Institute of Personnel and Development (2015). Harassment and bullying at work. Retrieved 25 October 2015 from http://www.cipd.co.uk/hr-resources/factsheets/harassment-bullying-at-work.aspx

259 https://www.centreformentalhealth.org.uk/what-ips

260 https://www.essex.ac.uk/-/media/documents/business/ecc-report_final_august-2018.pdf?la=en

261 Bertram, M. (2019). Mental health, social inclusion and the development of vocational services in the NHS – what can be learnt?. *Mental Health Review Journal, 24*(2), 133–143. doi:10.1108/MHRJ-09-2018-0027

262 Butterworth, P., Leach, L.S., Strazdins, L., Oleson, S.C., Rodgers, B. & Broom, D.H. (2011). The psychosocial quality of work determines whether employment has benefits for mental health: Results from a longitudinal national household panel survey. *Occupational and Environmental Medicine, Vol. 68*, 806–12.

263 Cooklin, A.R., Canterford, L., Strazdins, L. & Nicholson, J.M. (2011). Employment conditions and maternal postpartum mental health: Results from the longitudinal study of Australian Children. *Archives of Women's Mental Health, Vol. 14*, 217–25.

264 https://www.independent.co.uk/news/uk/home-news/disability-benefit-claimants-attempted-suicides-fitto-work-assessment-i-dan and https://digital.nhs.uk/data-and-information/publications/statistical/adultpsychiatric-morbidity-survey/adult-psychiatric-morbidity-survey-survey-of-mental-health-and-wellbeingengland-2014 iel-blake-job-centre-dwp-a8119286.html

265 Fryers, T. (2006). https://www.ncbi.nlm.nih.gov/pmc/articles/PMC1501011/

266 https://www.mentalhealth.org.uk/publications/how-to-in-later-life

267 https://www.studentsagainstdepression.org/

268 Aldridge, F. & Lavender, P. (2000). *The impact of learning on health.* Leicester: NIACE.

269 https://www.moneyandmentalhealth.org

270 Citizens' Advice https://www.citizensadvice.org.uk/

271 National Debt Line https://www.nationaldebtline.org/

272 National Institute for Health and Clinical Excellence (2018). *Depression: The NICE Guideline on the treatment and management of depression in adults* [NICE CG 90]. Accessed 13 September 2020 at https://www.nice.org.uk/guidance/cg90/evidence/full-guideline-pdf-4840934509

273 World Health Organization. (1992). *International statistical classification of diseases and related health problems* (10th rev.). (ICD-10). Geneva: WHO.

274 American Psychiatric Association. (2013). *Diagnostic and statistical manual of mental disorders* (5th edn). (DSM-5). Arlington, VA: American Psychiatric Publishing.

275 https://www.sign.ac.uk/assets/pat114_large_print.pdf

276 National Institute for Health and Care Excellence (2009). *Depression in adults – Recognition and management* [NICE CG 90]. Retrieved October 2014 from https://www.nice.org.uk/guidance/cg90

277 Hackman, C. Wilson, J., Perkins, A. & Zeilig, H. (2019). Collaborative diagnosis between clinician and patient: what it is and what to consider. *BJPsych Advances* (2019), page 1 of S. doi:10.1192/bia.2019.6

278 https://www.bps.org.uk/system/files/user-files/Division%20of%20Clinical%20Psychology/public/DCP%20Diagnosis.pdf

279 National Institute for Health and Care Excellence. (2009). *Depression in adults – Recognition and*

*management* [NICE CG 90]. Retrieved October 2014 from https://www.nice.org.uk/guidance/cg90

280 Jobst, A. et al. (2016). European Psychiatric Association Guidance on psychotherapy in chronic depression across Europe. *European Psychiatry, Volume 33*, 18–36. https://doi.org/10.1016/j.eurpsy.2015.12.003)

281 American Psychological Association, Guideline Development Panel for the Treatment of Depressive Disorders. (2019). *Clinical practice guideline for the treatment of depression across three age cohorts.* Retrieved from https://www.apa.org/depression-guideline/guideline.pdf.)

282 McPherson, S., Wicks, C. & Tercelli, I. (2020). Patient experiences of psychological therapy for depression: A qualitative metasynthesis. *BMC Psychiatry 20,* 313. https://doi.org/10.1186/s12888-020-02682-1

283 MIND (2013). We still need to talk: A report on accessing talking therapies. London: MIND publications. www.mind.org.uk/media/494424/we-still-need-to-talk_report.pdf

284 Deegan, P.E. (2001). Recovery as a self-directed process of healing and transformation. In C. Brown (Ed.) *Recovery and wellness: Models of hope and empowerment for people with mental illness* (pp.5–21). Philadelphia: Haworth Press.

285 Harper, D. & Moss, N. (2003). A different kind of chemistry? Reformulating 'formulation'. *Clinical Psychology, 25,* 6–10.

286 Butler, G. (1998). Clinical formulation. In A.S. Bellack & M. Hersen (Eds.) *Comprehensive clinical psychology, volume 6.* Oxford: Elsevier.

287 Moore, P, (2007). Formulation diagrams: Is there more than meets the eye? *Clinical Psychology Forum no 174 June 2007.*

288 https://thepsychologist.bps.org.uk/volume-30/september-2017/un-report-points-power-imbalances

289 Seikkula, J., Aaltonen, J., Alakare, B. et al. (2006). Five-year experience of first-episode nonaffective psychosis in open-dialogue approach: treatment principles, follow-up outcomes, and two case studies. *Psychotherapy Research, Vol. 16 No. 2*, 214–28. doi:10.1080/10503300500268490.

290 Paulson, J.F. & Bazemore, S.D. (2010). Prenatal and postpartum depression in fathers and its association with maternal depression: a meta-analysis. *J Am Med Assoc, 303,* 1961–1969. [PubMed]

291 O'Hara, M. & Swain, A. (2009). Rates and risk of postpartum depression: a meta-analysis. *Int Rev Psychiatry, 8,* 37–54.

292 Stein, A., Pearson, R., Goodman, S. et al. (2014). Effects of perinatal disorders on the fetus and child. *The Lancet, 384* (9956), 1800–1819.

293 Gellhorn, S. (Ed.) (2016). *Postnatal Depression and Maternal Mental Health: A handbook for frontline caregivers working with women with perinatal mental health difficulties.* Hove: Pavilion.

294 https://www.mind.org.uk/information-support/guides-to-support-and-services/advocacy/legal-rights-to-advocacy/

295 https://www.madinamerica.com/2015/10/id-rather-die-than-go-back-to-hospital-why-weneed-a-non-medical-crisis-house-in-every-town/

296 National Institute for Health and Care Excellence (2004). *Self-harm in over 8s: short-term management and prevention of recurrence* [NICE CG 16]. https://www.nice.org.uk/guidance/cg16/resources/selfharm-inover-8s-shortterm-management-and-prevention-of-recurrence-pdf-975268985029

297 Samaritans http://www.samaritans.org

298 Citizens' Advice https://www.citizensadvice.org.uk/

299 https://www.mind.org.uk/information-support/legal-rights/mental-capacity-act-2005/advancedecisions/#one

300 https://www.rethink.org/living-with-mental-illness/rights-restrictions/planning-your-care-advancestatements/about#diff

301 World Health Organization (2017). Depression and Other Common Mental Health Disorders: Global Health Estimates. WHO/MSD/MER/2017.2

302 Piketty, T. & Goldhammer, A. (2014). *Capital in the twenty-first century.* Cambridge Massachusetts: The Belknap Press of Harvard University Press.

303 Marmot, M., Allen, J., Boyce, T., Goldblatt, P. & Morrison, J. (2020). Health equity in England: The Marmot Review 10 years on. London: Institute of Health Equity. http://www.instituteofhealthequity.org/resources-reports/marmot-review-10-years-on

304 Wilkinson, R. & Pickett, K. (2009). *The spirit level: Why equality is better for everyone.* London: Penguin books.

305 Mitchell, A., Rub, S. & Wainwright, T. (2019). Demanding disruption: Extinction Rebellion and changing psychology. *Clinical Psychology Forum 319,* 28–33.

306 Australian Psychological Society (2016). *The climate change empowerment handbook.* https://www.psychology.org.au/for-the-public/Psychology-Topics/Climate-change-psychology

307 Menzies, Lyth I. (1959).The functions of social systems as a defence against anxiety: a report on a study of the nursing service of a general hospital. *Human Relations, 13,* 95–121. Reprinted in *Containing Anxiety in Institutions: Selected Essays, Vol 1.* Free Association Books, 1988.